PLOTINUS

ENNEAD II.5

THE *ENNEADS* OF PLOTINUS

With Philosophical Commentaries

Series Editors: John M. Dillon, Trinity College, Dublin and Andrew Smith, University College, Dublin

Also Available in the Series:

I.1: *What Is the Living Thing? What Is Man?* by Gerard O'Daly

I.6: *On Beauty* by Andrew Smith

II.4: *On Matter* by Anthony A. Long

II.5: *On What Is Potentially and What Actually* by Cinzia Arruzza

II.9: *Against the Gnostics* by Sebastian Ramon Philipp Gertz

IV.3–4.29: *Problems Concerning the Soul* by John M. Dillon & H. J. Blumenthal

IV.4.30–45 & IV.5: *Problems Concerning the Soul* by Gary Gurtler

IV.7: *On the Immortality of the Soul* by Barrie Fleet

IV.8: *On the Descent of the Soul Into Bodies* by Barrie Fleet

V.1: *On the Three Primary Levels of Reality* by Eric D. Perl

V.5: *That the Intelligibles are not External to Intellect, and on the Good* by Lloyd P. Gerson

VI.4 & VI.5: *On the Presence of Being, One and the Same, Everywhere as a Whole* by Eyjólfur Emilsson & Steven Strange

VI.8: *On the Voluntary and on the Free Will of the One* by Kevin Corrigan and John D. Turner

VI.9: *On the Good or the One* by Stephen R. L. Clark

Forthcoming Titles in the Series Include:

I.2: *On Virtues* by Suzanne Stern-Gillet

I.3: *On Dialectic* by Pauliina Remes

I.4: *On Well-Being* by Kieran McGroarty

I.5: *On Whether Well-Being Increases with Time* by Danielle A. Laney

I.8: *On the Nature and Source of Evil* by Anne Sheppard

I.9: *On Going Out of the Body* by Suzanne Stern-Gilet

II.1: *On the Heavens* by Andrew Smith

II.6: *On Substance, or On Quality* by Damien Caluori

II.7: *On Complete Blending* by Robert Goulding

II.8: *On Sight* by Robert Goulding

III.5: *On Love* by Sara Magrin

III.6: *On Impassibility* by Eleni Perdikouri

III.7: *On Eternity and Time* by László Bene

III.8: *On Nature and Contemplation* by George Karamanolis

IV.6: *On Sense-Perception and Memory* by Peter Lautner

IV.9: *If All Souls are One* by Eyjólfur Emilsson

V.2, **V.4**, and **V.6**: *On the One and Intellect* by Eleni Perdikouri

V.3: *On the Knowing Hypostases* by Marie-Élise Zovko

V.9: *On Intellect, Ideas, and Being* by Matthias Vorwerk

VI.1–2: *On the Genera of Being (I+II)* by Damien Caluori & Regina Füchslin

VI.3: *On the Genera of Being (III)* by Riccardo Chiaradonna

VI.7: *The Forms and the Good* by Nicholas Banner

PLOTINUS
ENNEAD II.5

On What Is Potentially and What Actually

Translation with an Introduction and Commentary

CINZIA ARRUZZA

PARMENIDES PUBLISHING

Las Vegas | Zurich | Athens

PARMENIDES PUBLISHING
Las Vegas | Zurich | Athens

This edition published in 2015 by Parmenides Publishing
in the United States of America

ISBN soft cover: 978-1-930972-63-6
ISBN e-Book: 978-1-930972-90-2

Library of Congress Cataloging-in-Publication Data

Plotinus.
[Ennead. II, 5. English]
Ennead II.5 : on what is potentially and what actually / Plotinus ; translation with an introduction and commentary, Cinzia Arruzza. -- 1st edition.
pages cm. -- (The Enneads of Plotinus with philosophical commentaries)
Includes bibliographical references and index.
ISBN 978-1-930972-63-6 (pbk. : alk. paper) -- ISBN 978-1-930972-90-2 (ebook)
1. Plotinus. Ennead. II, 5. 2. Power (Philosophy)--Early works to 1800. I. Arruzza, Cinzia, translator, commentator. II. Title. III. Title: On what is potentially and what actually.
B693.E52E5 2015c
186'.4--dc23

2015020893

Typeset in Warnock and Futura by Parmenides Publishing
Printed digitally by Integrated Books International (IBI), Chicago, IL

www.parmenides.com

Contents

To Anna, Daniela, Euree, and Marta

Introduction to the Series With a Brief Outline of the Life and Thought of Plotinus (205–270 CE)

PLOTINUS WAS BORN IN 205 CE in Egypt of Greek-speaking parents. He attended the philosophical schools in Alexandria where he would have studied Plato (427–347 BCE), Aristotle (384–322 BCE), the Stoics and Epicureans as well as other Greek philosophical traditions. He began his serious philosophical education, however, relatively late in life, at the age of twenty-seven and was deeply impressed by the Platonist Ammonius Saccas about whom we, unfortunately, know very little, but with whom Plotinus studied for some eleven years. Even our knowledge of Plotinus' life is limited to what we can glean from Porphyry's introduction to his edition of his philosophical treatises, an account colored by Porphyry's own concerns. After completing his studies in Alexandria Plotinus attempted, by joining a military expedition of the Roman emperor Gordian III, to make contact with the

Brahmins in order to learn something of Indian thought. Unfortunately Gordian was defeated and killed (244). Plotinus somehow managed to extract himself and we next hear of him in Rome where he was able to set up a school of philosophy in the house of a high-ranking Roman lady by the name of Gemina. It is, perhaps, surprising that he had no formal contacts with the Platonic Academy in Athens, which was headed at the time by Longinus, but Longinus was familiar with his work, partly at least through Porphyry who had studied in Athens. The fact that it was Rome where Plotinus set up his school may be due to the originality of his philosophical activity and to his patrons. He clearly had some influential contacts, not least with the philhellenic emperor Gallienus (253–268), who may also have encouraged his later failed attempt to set up a civic community based on Platonic principles in a ruined city in Campania.

Plotinus' school was, like most ancient schools of philosophy, relatively small in scale, but did attract distinguished students from abroad and from the Roman upper classes. It included not only philosophers but also politicians and members of the medical profession who wished to lead the philosophical life. His most famous student was Porphyry (233–305) who, as a relative latecomer to the school, persuaded him to put into writing the results of his seminars. It is almost certain that we possess most, if not all, of his written output, which represents his mature thought, since he didn't commence writing until the age of forty-eight. The school seemingly had inner and outer circles, and Plotinus himself was clearly an inspiring and sympathetic teacher who took a deep interest in the philosophical and spiritual progress of his students. Porphyry tells us that when he was suffering from severe depression Plotinus straight away visited him in his lodgings to help him. His concern for others is also illustrated by the fact that he was entrusted with the personal education of many orphans and the care of their property and careers. The reconciliation of this worldly involvement with the encouragement to lead a life of contemplation is encapsulated in Porphyry's comment that "he was present to himself and others at the same time."

The *Enneads* of Plotinus is the edition of his treatises arranged by his pupil Porphyry who tried to put shape to the collection he had inherited by organizing it into six sets of nine treatises (hence the name *"Enneads")* that led the reader through the levels of Plotinus' universe, from the physical world to Soul, Intellect and, finally, to the highest principle, the One. Although Plotinus undoubtedly had a clearly structured metaphysical system by the time he began committing himself to expressing his thought in written form, the treatises themselves are not systematic expositions, but rather explorations of particular themes and issues raised in interpreting Plato and other philosophical texts read in the School. In fact, to achieve his neat arrangement Porphyry was sometimes driven even to dividing certain treatises (e.g., III.2–3; IV.3–5, and VI.4–5).

Although Plotinus' writings are not transcripts of his seminars, but are directed to the reader, they do, nevertheless, convey the sort of lively debate that he encouraged in his school. Frequently he takes for granted that a particular set of ideas is already familiar as having been treated in an earlier seminar that may or may not be found in the written text. For this reason it is useful for the reader to have some idea of the main philosophical principles of his system as they can be extracted from the *Enneads* as a whole.

Plotinus regarded himself as a faithful interpreter of Plato whose thought lies at the core of his entire project. But Plato's thought, whilst definitive, does according to Plotinus require careful exposition and clarification, often in the light of other thinkers such as Aristotle and the Stoics. It is because of this creative application of different traditions of ancient thought to the interpretation of Plato that Plotinus' version of Platonism became, partly through the medium of later Platonists such as Porphyry, Iamblichus (245–325), and Proclus (412–485), an influential source and way of reading both Plato and Aristotle in the Middle Ages, the Renaissance, and up to the early 19th century, when scholars first began to differentiate Plato and "Neoplatonism." His thought, too, provided early Christian theologians of the Latin and particularly of the Byzantine tradition, with a rich variety of metaphysical concepts with which to explore and express difficult doctrinal ideas. His fashioning of Plato's ideas into a consistent metaphysical structure, though no longer accepted as a uniquely valid way of approaching Plato, was influential in promoting the notion of metaphysical systems in early modern philosophy. More recently increasing interest has centered on his exploration of the self, levels of consciousness, and his expansion of discourse beyond the levels of normal ontology to the examination of what lies both above and beneath being. His thought continues to challenge us when confronted with the issue of man's nature and role in the universe and of the extent and limitations of human knowledge.

Whilst much of Plotinus' metaphysical structure is recognizably an interpretation of Plato it is an interpretation that is not always immediately obvious just because it is filtered through several centuries of developing Platonic thought, itself already overlaid with important concepts drawn from other schools. It is, nevertheless, useful as a starting point to see how Plotinus attempts to bring coherence to what he believed to be a comprehensive worldview expressed in the Platonic dialogues. The Platonic Forms are central. They become for him an intelligible universe that is the source and model of the physical universe. But aware of Aristotle's criticism of the Platonic Forms as lifeless causes he takes on board Aristotle's concept of god as a self-thinker to enable him to identify this intelligible universe as a divine Intellect that thinks itself as the Forms or Intelligibles. The doctrine of the Forms as the thoughts of god had already entered Platonism, but not as the rigorously argued identity that Plotinus proposed. Moreover the Intelligibles, since they are identical with Intellect, are themselves actively intellectual; they are intellects. Thus Plato's world of Forms has become a complex and dynamic intelligible universe in which unity and plurality, stability, and activity are reconciled.

Now although the divine Intellect is one it also embraces plurality, both because its thoughts, the Intelligibles, are many and because it may itself be analyzed into thinker and thought. Its unity demands a further principle, which is the cause of its unity. This principle, which is the cause of all unity and being but does not possess unity or being in itself, he calls the One, an interpretation of the Idea of the Good in Plato's *Republic* that is "beyond being" and that may be seen as the simple (hence "one") source of all reality. We thus have the first two of what subsequently became known as the three Hypostases, the One, Intellect, and Soul, the last of which acts as an intermediary between the intelligible and physical universes. This last Hypostasis takes on all the functions of transmitting form and life that may be found in Plato, although Plato himself does not always make such a clear distinction between soul and intellect.

Thus the One is the ultimate source of all, including this universe, which is then prefigured in Intellect and transmitted through Soul to become manifest as our physical universe. Matter, which receives imperfectly this expression, is conceived not as an independently existing counter-principle, a dangerously dualist notion, but is in a sense itself a product of the One, a kind of non-being that, while being nothing specific in itself, nevertheless is not simply not there.

But this procession from an ultimate principle is balanced by a return movement at each level of reality that fully constitutes itself only when it turns back in contemplation of its producer. And so the whole of reality is a dynamic movement of procession and return, except for matter, which has no life of its own to make this return; it is inert. This movement of return, which may be traced back to the force of "love" in Plato or Aristotle's final cause, is characterized by Plotinus as a cognitive activity, a form of contemplation, weaker at each successive level, from Intellect through discursive reasoning to the merest image of rational order as expressed in the objects of the physical universe.

The human individual mirrors this structure to which we are all related at each level. For each of us has a body and soul, an intellect, and even something within us that relates to the One. While it is the nature of soul to give life to body, the higher aspect of our soul also has aspirations toward intellect, the true self, and even beyond. This urge to return corresponds to the cosmic movement of return. But the tension between soul's natural duty to body and its origins in the intelligible can be, for the individual, a source of fracture and alienation in which the soul becomes over-involved and overwhelmed by the body and so estranged from its true self. Plotinus encourages us to make the return or ascent, but at the same time attempts to resolve the conflict of duties by reconciling the two-fold nature of soul as life-giving and contemplative.

This is the general framework within which important traditional philosophical issues are encountered, discussed and resolved, but always in a spirit of inquiry and ongoing debate. Issues are frequently encountered in several different contexts, each angle providing a different insight. The nature of the soul and its relationship to the body is examined at length (IV) using the Aristotelian distinctions of levels of soul (vegetative, growth, sensitive, rational) whilst maintaining the immortal nature of the transcendent soul in Platonic terms. The active nature of the soul in sense-perception is maintained to preserve the principle that incorporeals cannot be affected by corporeal reality. A vigorous discussion (VI.4 and 5) on the general nature of the relationship of incorporeals to body explores in every detail and in great depth the way in which incorporeals act on body. A universe that is the product of design is reconciled with the freedom of the individual. And, not least, the time-bound nature of the physical universe and human reason is grounded in the life of Intellect, which subsists in eternity. Sometimes, however, Plotinus seems to break outside the framework of traditional metaphysics: the nature of matter and the One, each as non-being, though in a different sense, strains the terminology and structure of traditional ontology; and the attempt to reconcile the role of the individual soul within the traditional Platonic distinction of transcendent and immanent reality leads to a novel exploration of the nature of the self, the "I."

It is this restless urge for exploration and inquiry that lends to the treatises of Plotinus their philosophical vitality. Whilst presenting us with a rich and complexly coherent system, he constantly engages us in philosophical inquiry. In this way each treatise presents us with new ideas and fresh challenges. And, for Plotinus, every philosophical engagement is not just a mental exercise but also contributes to the rediscovery of the self and our reintegration with the source of all being, the Platonic aim of "becoming like god."

While Plotinus, like Plato, always wishes to engage his audience to reflect for themselves, his treatises are not easy reading, partly no doubt because his own audience was already familiar with many of his basic ideas and, more importantly, had been exposed in his seminars to critical readings of philosophical texts that have not survived to our day. Another problem is that the treatises do not lay out his thought in a systematic way but take up specific issues, although always the whole system may be discerned in the background. Sometimes, too, the exact flow of thought is difficult to follow because of an often condensed mode of expression.

Because we are convinced that Plotinus has something to say to us today, we have launched this series of translations and commentaries as a means of opening up the text to readers with an interest in grappling with the philosophical issues revealed by an encounter with Plotinus' own words and arguments. Each volume will contain a new translation, careful summaries of the arguments and structure of the treatise, and a philosophical commentary that will aim to throw light on the philosophical meaning and import of the text.

John M. Dillon
Andrew Smith

Abbreviations

Armstrong Armstrong, A. H. 1966–1982. *Plotinus, Enneads.* Greek Text with English Translation and Introductions. Cambridge, MA: Loeb.

Bréhier Bréhier, É. 1924–1938. *Plotin, Ennéades.* Greek Text and French Translation with Introductions and Notes. Paris: Les Belles Lettres.

Creuzer Creuzer, G. F. 1835. *Plotini Enneades.* Greek Text, with Marsilio Ficino's Latin Translation and Commentary. Oxford: E Typographeo Academico.

Denniston Denniston, J. D. 1954. *The Greek Particles.* Oxford: Clarendon Press.

HS_1 Henry, P. and Schwyzer, H.-R. 1951–1973. *Plotini Opera* I-III (editio maior). Paris: Desclée de Brouwer et Cie.

HS_2	Henry, P. and Schwyzer, H.-R. 1964–1982. *Plotini Opera* I-III (editio minor, with revised text). Oxford: Clarendon Press.
HS_3	Henry, P. and Schwyzer, H.-R. 1973. *Addenda et Corrigenda ad textum et apparatum lectionum*. In HS_1, t. III.
HS_4	Henry, P. and Schwyzer, H.-R. 1982. *Addenda et Corrigenda ad textum et apparatum lectionum*. In HS_2, t. III.
HS_5	Schwyzer, H.-R. 1987. "Corrigenda ad Plotini Textum." *Museum Helveticum* 44, 191–210.
Kirchhoff	Kirchhoff, A. 1856. *Plotini Opera*. Leipzig: Teubner.
LS	Long, A. A., Sedley D. N., trans. 1987. *The Hellenistic Philosophers, Volume 1: Translation of the Principal Sources, with Philosophical Commentary*. Cambridge: Cambridge University Press.
SVF	Von Arnim, H., ed. 1905. *Stoicorum Veterum Fragmenta*. Leipzig: Teubner.

Acknowledgments

I WOULD LIKE TO EXPRESS my deep gratitude to John Dillon and Andrew Smith for their invaluable comments on the introduction, commentary, and translation and to the editorial team of Parmenides Press for their excellent work. I'm particularly grateful to Eyjólfur Kjalar Emilsson for his advice on a draft of this text, and to Christoph Horn and the Alexander von Humboldt Stiftung for providing me with the best possible conditions to conduct my research on potentiality and actuality in Plotinus' *Enneads* between 2008 and 2010. I am grateful to the participants in the June 2011 Dublin Plotinus Colloquium organized by John Dillon and Andrew Smith: the conversations and ideas we exchanged throughout that event were of great help to my work. I want to express many thanks to my student, Marcello Kilani, for editing my English. I'm also grateful to my colleagues at the Philosophy Department of the New School for Social Research for their support, kindness and wisdom. Finally, I am indebted to four women, Marta Cristiani, Anna Schriefl, Euree Song, and Daniela P. Taormina: my deepest gratitude for our many philosophical conversations, for their support and friendship over the years. This book is dedicated to them.

Introduction to the Treatise

In classical Greek *dunamis* was a loose word for power, understood to have a variety of possible meanings, including physical strength, political power, divine power, natural capacities, and the sense-faculties. The term entered the philosophical vocabulary with a more specific meaning already through Plato, but it was with Aristotle that it acquired, together with *energeia* (actuality), the strong technical meaning it has maintained, with variations, throughout the subsequent philosophical tradition. With Aristotle, indeed, *dunamis* and *energeia* came to indicate two ways of being, capable of explaining motion, causality, change and hylomorphism, as well as sensation, sense-perception, and the operations of the soul.

The significance of the notions of actuality and potentiality in Plotinus' thought can hardly be overestimated. Throughout the *Enneads, dunamis*, understood as "active power," together with the doctrine of double *energeia*, are crucial to understanding the specific causality of intelligible realities and of the relation of participation between intelligible and sensible realms. "Power of everything" (*dunamis pantōn*) or "infinite power" (*apeiros dunamis*) define the One's generative capacity and explain how everything comes from the One without the One being affected by its own overflowing into the totality of things. *Energeia* defines the nature of intelligible realities, whose being is the outcome of their self-constituting activity. The *dunameis* of the soul explain both the diverse operations of the soul and its capacity to ensoul, govern, shape and move sensible bodies. Finally, *dunamis* and *energeia* are central to Plotinus' understanding of phenomena of change in the sensible realm.

While he inherited the technical, philosophical use of the terms *dunamis* and *energeia* from the Aristotelian tradition, Plotinus was not an Aristotelian. He radically revised Aristotle's notion of potentiality and actuality, adapting them to his system of thought, and transforming them into a new and original conceptual device, one where influences from Platonic and Stoic sources play an important role. Plotinus, indeed, conceived of his philosophy as the correct interpretation of Plato's dialogues, and Porphyry informs us of the relevance of Aristotle's and Stoic philosophy to his thought: "His writings, however, are full of concealed Stoic and Peripatetic doctrines. Aristotle's *Metaphysics*, in particular, is concentrated in them."[1]

The relevance of these sources is the reason why it will be useful, before addressing Plotinus' own conception of actuality and potentiality in general and in *Ennead* II.5 [25] in particular, to give a short survey of the two notions in the previous philosophical tradition and to examine briefly the use of *dunamis* in Plato and in the Stoics, as well as Aristotle's doctrine of potentiality and actuality.

Dunamis in Plato

The terms *dunamis, dunaton, dunasthai* recur throughout Plato's dialogues with an array of meanings linked either to ordinary language or to specific technical usage: the power of magnets (*Ion* 533d3), the power of rhetoric (*Gorgias* 456a5), the capacity for pleasure (*Philebus* 44c7; d4), political power (*Republic* 473d3; 494c2; 567b3; 591a8; *Protagoras* 317a3; *Statesman* 304d9; 310b7), sense-faculties and intellectual faculties (*Theaetetus* 84e8; 185c3), but also the "root" and "power" in geometry (*Theaetetus* 147d).[2] While Plato's use of these terms is not always rigorous, there are at least two passages, from the *Republic* and the *Sophist*, where we find not only a more technical use of the

1 Porphyry, *Life of Plotinus* 14.4–7; translation: Armstrong.

2 For a more complete list of meanings and references see Cleary (2013, 253–254).

terms related to *dunamis*, but also a philosophical elaboration of them which makes *dunamis* a decisive concept for understanding being, movement, and knowledge.

Republic

Generally speaking, *dunamis* can be understood as the principle of movement, as the capacity to act and to be acted upon, attributed to natural and artificial objects, to inanimate or animate beings, to activities, and perhaps even to Forms. In *Republic* 477c1–4 we find the following definition: "We will assert that powers are a certain class of beings by means of which we are capable of what we are capable, and also everything else is capable of whatever it is capable. For example, I say sight and hearing are powers, if perchance you understand the form of which I wish to speak" (translation: Bloom). Socrates provides this definition within the context of the distinction between knowledge (*epistēmē*) and opinion (*doxa*), which he has described as two different kinds of powers a few lines earlier (477b7–8). This distinction relies on two criteria, the operation of a thing and the object to which this operation applies: knowledge and opinion are two different powers because they do different things, to know and to opine, and are set over two different classes of object, the things which truly are and are always the same, and the things that partake in being and non-being alike (477c6–478b1).

From this passage we learn that powers are kinds of being (*genos ti tōn ontōn*, 477c1). As we will see, in the *Sophist* we find an inverted definition, namely that being in itself is a *dunamis*. Both descriptions convey the indissoluble relationship between being and power, in the sense that *dunamis* is an essential dimension of each and all beings. Now, powers are those classes of beings that enable things both to operate and have effects, and to be the passive objects of operations. These powers are differential, in the sense that each being will have a different power according to the operations that being can perform and the objects on which it can perform them. The same holds for passive capacities: as my eyes do not have the power to be affected by sounds, so my ears do not have the power to be affected by colors. Indeed, this insistence on the object of an operation highlights another fundamental aspect of *dunamis*, namely that a capacity to be acted upon, or passive capacity, must correspond to the capacity to act: to act and to be acted upon are correlative terms.

Sophist

In the *Sophist* we can find the philosophically most interesting passage concerning the meaning of *dunamis* and its relation to being. The passage comes in the context of the Stranger's examination of different theories about being and non-being: those of the pluralists, of the monists, of the materialists, and of the "Friends of Forms." After focusing on the materialists, whom he refutes by forcing them to admit that at least some immaterial realities, such as virtues, do exist (246c–248a), the Stranger addresses the Friends of Forms' rigid distinction and separation between intelligible and sensible reality and their claim that movement should be excluded from being (248a–249c). In order to challenge this separation, the Stranger begins by giving the following definition of being: "We took it as a sufficient definition of *beings* that the capacity be present in a thing to do something or have something done to it, to or by even the smallest thing or degree" (248c4–5, translation: White). By defining beings as *dunamis*, the Stranger is giving a dynamic and relational account of them, as the being of a thing is defined by its capacity to relate to other things either by acting or by being acted upon.[3] This definition, however, is not accepted by the Friends of Forms, who attribute the capacity to do something or have something done to it only to becoming, but not to being. Indeed by accepting that being has or is essentially a *dunamis* they would be forced to introduce movement into being. This is precisely the Stranger's goal against the Friends of Forms. He then goes on to ask whether knowing is doing something: for if this is the case, then what is known is the passive object

3 See Fronterotta (2008, 194).

of the act of knowing and it is acted upon. The Friends of Forms cannot accept this suggestion either. Indeed, the proper object of knowledge is being, and by accepting that knowing and being known equate to acting and being acted upon, they would again introduce passivity and change into being (248d1–e5). The Stranger, however, rejects this position as absurd: "But for heaven's sake, are we going to be convinced that it's true that change, life, soul, and intelligence are not present in *that which wholly is* (*tōi pantelōs onti*), and that it neither lives nor thinks, but stays changeless, solemn, and holy, without any understanding?" (248e7–249a2, translation: White).

The whole passage is extremely controversial and has been interpreted in different ways. Indeed, what does it mean that being is *dunamis*? And what are the consequences of this assumption for Plato's theory of Forms? Did he change his mind about the immutability and eternity of the Forms? We can distinguish three possible interpretations of *Sophist* 248e7–249a2. According to the first, in the *Parmenides* Plato had abandoned his previous view about the Forms, in order to endorse an understanding of the Forms as concepts subject to change: the *Sophist* passage, then, confirms this development in Plato's philosophy. The second interpretive line argues for the opposite view: Plato has not changed his mind about the Forms, which remain unchangeable and eternal. These two opposite interpretations are based on two different readings of *to pantelōs on* at lines 248e8–249a1: this expression can, indeed, be translated either in an intensional way, as "what wholly is," meaning the intelligible being, the Forms, or in an extensional way, as "being in its totality," which would then include both intelligible and sensible being. In the latter case, the Stranger's point is not that we need to attribute movement to the Forms, but rather that we cannot exclude movement from the totality of being, because by doing so we would also exclude life, the soul and thought.[4] This also implies that the *dunamis koinōnias*, the capacity for association, which the Stranger attributes to the Forms as they are in relation with each other, is different from the *dunamis* of the sensible realm, for it does not entail any change or movement.[5]

A third interpretive line on our passage has been offered by Fronterotta[6] and it is worth spending some time on it, because it is a reading of the relation between *dunamis* and being that is close to the Middle Platonic and Neoplatonic interpretations of the relation between intelligible Forms and the sensible world. It can, therefore, help shed some light on the way Plotinus might have read this passage of the *Sophist*. According to Fronterotta, in the *Sophist* Plato offers an ontology based on a dynamic and participative notion of being. This dynamic and relational

4 See Brisson (2008, 182).

5 See Brisson (2008, 184–185).

6 See Fronterotta (2001) and Fronterotta (2008).

aspect belongs originally and essentially to the being of everything, including the Forms: it characterizes their original ontological structure. Indeed, for Fronterotta, *to pantelōs on* does refer to the intelligible being, and it indicates, both intensionally and extensionally, the domain of the things that really are. However, the movement we attribute to intelligible beings should not be understood as a concrete, spatial movement, but rather as a pure intelligible movement. On the same line, Forms *are* affected, but the way they are affected is purely formal.

On this account, then, we need to attribute fully to the Forms the capacity to act and to be acted upon. This *dunamis* is the source of the constitutively relational structure of the Forms: indeed, their reciprocal communication, *koinōnia*, is a consequence of their capacity to communicate with each other. Now, if the Forms are *dunameis*, one might draw the consequence that the participation between sensible and intelligible beings can also be explained precisely on the basis of the notion of *dunamis*. On this account the Forms would be efficient causes of the sensible beings that partake of them. It is true that Plato never explicitly took this position in the dialogues, but subsequent Platonists, from Philo to Plotinus, did interpret the relation of participation in this way.

Potentiality and Actuality in Aristotle

The most relevant texts concerning Aristotle's treatment of potentiality and actuality can be found in the *Metaphysics*, in the *Physics*, and in *On the Soul* (*De Anima*). It is most likely that these three works have all been important sources for Plotinus' own elaboration on this theme.

Dunamis

In *Metaphysics* 5.12.1019a15–32, Aristotle identifies four different meanings of *dunamis*, all of which relate to ordinary ways of speaking about potentiality. The first meaning conveys the active and productive sense of power, as the power of doing something and having effects: *dunamis* is the principle of movement and of change which is "in another thing or in the same thing *qua* other" (1019a15–16). The second definition describes *dunamis* as the capacity to be acted upon, as the passive capacity to be affected (1019a19–20). The following two definitions convey two more specific meanings of *dunamis*, as the power of acting or being acted upon well (*kalōs*) or according to a deliberate choice (*kata proairesin*), and as impassibility or the capacity to resist corruption and destruction (1019a23–32). Alexander of Aphrodisias interprets these last kinds of *dunamis* as two different sorts of *hexis*, that is, as two acquired states. For example, we say that someone is able to speak not only when he has the natural capacity of doing so, but also when he has an acquired capacity to speak well (for example, because he has been trained in rhetoric). The same holds for the capacity of not being affected in a negative way.[7] In a sense, then, having a *dunamis* means having the capacity either to operate changes or to be affected both in a negative or in a positive way; in another sense, though, *dunamis* indicates only a capacity for perfection or for positive changes.

These indications are elaborated upon and further articulated in the first part of Book 9 (chapters 1–5), while the second part of the book (chapters 6–9) elaborates upon a more technical and metaphysical use of the terms *dunamis* and *energeia*. Starting from the definition of *dunamis* as the principle of change and movement, Aristotle restates the distinction between active and passive potentiality. He then operates a further distinction among active powers, that between rational and irrational active powers. The first ones include the arts and the productive knowledges and they can have opposite effects. For example, the art of medicine has the power either to heal or to make sick. On the contrary, irrational powers, such as those of natural elements, can have only one kind of effect inherent to their nature (*Metaphysics* 9.2.1046b4–7). He then goes on to list a series of conditions under which something

7 Alexander of Aphrodisias, *On Aristotle's Metaphysics* 5.390.

can be spoken of as being in potentiality: it is not only possible, but even necessary, to reject the Megarian claim that something is not in potentiality before its actualization and regardless of whether the actualization can take place; something can be said to be in potentiality only when the possibility to actualize this potentiality is present; things are in potentiality in a determinate way, at a determinate time and with respect to a determinate thing, and not in general.[8]

In the more technical sense discussed starting from chapter 6, the concept of potentiality defines a mode of being and plays an important role in the definition of substance. Here potential being cannot be defined independently of actual being, for, since we say that everything which is potentiality has the capacity of changing to actuality, *energeia* is conceptually prior to *dunamis*. We will discuss the meaning of *energeia* later in more detail. Here it is sufficient to say that if *energeia* is the full existence of a thing, which includes its form, then *dunamis* is matter (1048a32–b9). If we take a bronze statue, for example, bronze will be the potential being of the compound, while the statue itself, with its immanent form, will be the actual being. In the passage from potentiality to actuality, the matter "bronze" receives a form and therefore becomes a statue. But *dunamis* can also refer to a capacity to act

8 These conditions will be discussed in detail in the Commentary.

or to do something as opposed to the activity itself or to the final outcome of the activity. For example, seeing an object is the *energeia* of the faculty of sight, while a house is the actualization of the capacity to build.

The meaning of *dunamis* as faculty is elaborated upon in *On the Soul*, where it plays a crucial role in explaining both sensation and thought. Sensation can be either potential (e.g., the faculty of sight) or actual (e.g., seeing): this is so because sensation takes place when the activity of a sensible object acts upon the proper sense-organ. For example, the power of hearing is actualized into actual hearing, when an object produces a sound that acts upon the sense organ. This means that we can have the capacity of hearing but not be exercising it, for example where there are no sounds to be heard (*On the Soul* 3.425b–426a). Actual sensation, then, is a kind of alteration; however, it is an alteration that preserves and does not destroy that which is potential (*On the Soul* 2.417b). The same holds for actual intellectual knowledge. Indeed, learning and acquiring knowledge can also be understood as actualizations of the capacity to learn. This capacity belongs to what it means to be a human being, it is implied in the *genos* human being, and its actualization requires an alteration from a condition of ignorance to the possession of knowledge: in this passage, the previous state, ignorance, is destroyed by the change and we have an alteration *qua* passage from contrary to contrary, from ignorance to knowledge. The possession of knowledge, however, can also be distinguished from its actual exercise, and in this sense it is a faculty or power as opposed to the *energeia* corresponding to its actual use. The passage from the possession to the actual use of knowledge is a very peculiar kind of alteration, comparable to that which takes place in the case of actual sensation: it entails the preservation of what is potential (*On the Soul* 2.5.417b).[9] And indeed, in *On Sense and Sensibilia* (*De Sensu et Sensibili*) 4.441b22, Aristotle clarifies that the activity of sense-perception is analogous not to the process of acquiring knowledge, but rather to exercising the knowledge that has already been acquired.

Energeia and Entelecheia

As we have said, the actualization of a *dunamis* can be either an actual existing thing or an activity. Aristotle distinguishes between two kinds of activities, complete and incomplete. Complete activities are those which do not have an aim outside themselves and in which there is a coincidence between the aim of the activity and the activity itself. For example, thinking or seeing are full actualizations of the corresponding faculties. Incomplete activities are those which have an end outside themselves and are defined by this external end: for example, building

9 This point will be discussed in more detail in the *Commentary*.

is an incomplete activity as it is oriented toward an external goal, that is, an actually existing house (*Metaphysics* 9.6.1048b18–35). In *Physics* 3.2.201b–202a Aristotle refers to this distinction in order to discuss the nature of natural movement (*kinēsis*), which he recognizes as being difficult to grasp: movement is here defined as an imperfect activity or as a qualified kind of activity, namely an activity directed toward an external goal and incomplete in itself. Natural movement can be fully considered as an actuality only in the sense of being the actuality of a mobile object *qua* mobile. This definition of movement as incomplete activity (*energeia atelēs*) will be explicitly challenged by Plotinus in VI.1 [42] 16, where Plotinus argues in favor of a distinction between movement as a cause of empirical phenomena, and the empirical and quantitative phenomena of movement in themselves. According to Plotinus, the definition of incomplete activity can be applied to empirical processes, but it cannot be applied to their cause: in this sense, then, movement is complete.[10]

To go back to the double way in which a *dunamis* can be actualized, in *Metaphysics* 9 Aristotle explains that *energeia* can indicate both the existence of a thing and an activity in the sense of the exercise of a power or capacity. As a matter of fact, though, he coined two different terms to refer to the correlative of *dunamis*: *energeia* and

10 See Chiaradonna (2002) and Chiaradonna (2008).

entelecheia. As Aristotle's usage of these two terms is not consistent, it is difficult to understand what the difference between the two might be, and even their etymology is controversial. Stephen Menn's hypothesis on this subject is that whereas the only meaning of *entelecheia* is "actuality," *energeia* was originally meant to indicate "activity," but then it came to be used by Aristotle himself to refer to both actuality and activity. This explains why Aristotle oscillates in his use of the two terms. For example, in *Metaphysics* 9 and 12 he tends to resort to the term *energeia* instead of *entelecheia* in order to refer to actuality, while he avoids such usage of *energeia* in his physical treatises.[11]

The term *entelecheia* plays a particular role in Aristotle's definition of the soul and of its relation to the body. In *On the Soul* 2.412a20–412b1 the soul is defined first as the substance or form of a body, and then as the actuality (*entelecheia*) of a body, and more specifically as the first actuality. The soul is defined as the first actuality of a natural body potentially possessing life, because it is analogous to the possession of knowledge as compared to the exercise of knowledge: the presence of the soul is what enables the body to act by making of it a living body. In the *Enneads*, Plotinus uses the term *entelecheia* only in the context of his discussion of the soul, where he rejects Aristotle's definition and defends against it the Platonic

11 See Menn (1994).

account of the immortality and independence of the soul from the body.[12]

As we have said, in *Metaphysics* 12 Aristotle tends to use the term *energeia* to indicate actuality. Here we find a very important discussion of the nature of the first principle. Aristotle first explains that, while actuality should be understood as both the form, insofar as this is separable, and the compound of matter and form, potentiality is matter, the actualization of which is possible, but not necessary. In other words, what characterizes being in potentiality is the fact that it is possible for it not to change from potentiality to actuality. This is the reason why being in potentiality is incompatible both with eternal substances and with eternal movement. Aristotle's conclusion, then, is that eternal substances do not have any potential being, and therefore do not have any matter: they must rather be pure acts (*Metaphysics* 12.6.1071b–1072a). The first principle, named by Aristotle "the unmoved mover" in order to indicate in it the original cause of every movement, is a principle the being of which (*ousia*) is an act itself (*energeia*). Here Aristotle restates the ontological priority of act over potentiality, as act is the cause of movement and therefore it is what brings to actuality something in potentiality. Since it is the first principle, the unmoved mover must be engaged in the highest possible

12 See, for example, *Enneads* IV.7 [2] 8[5].

activity; this is why in *Metaphysics* 12.7.1072b we discover that the first mover is an intellect (*nous*) thinking itself. This thinking activity (*noēsis*) is eternal and always in full possession of its object of thought.

Dunamis and Logos in the Stoics

The ancient Stoics did not take up Aristotle's systematization of the notions of potentiality and actuality and did not integrate it into their system of thought. However, one could hardly understand Stoic physics if one removed from it the fundamental idea that everything that is is capable either of acting or of being acted upon. Indeed, as emphasized by Brunschwig, the Stoics shared with Plato the "dynamic" criterion of existence as developed in the *Sophist*. Here, when discussing the materialist theses in the famous "Battle of the Giants," the Stranger of Elea attributed to the materialists the belief that the only existing beings are those who can offer resistance to touch, that is, bodies. The Stoics combined this claim with the general criterion that only things that are can act or be acted upon and reached the conclusion that only bodies can satisfy the general criterion of existence: "Zeno also differed from the same philosophers [Platonists and Peripatetics] in thinking that it was totally impossible that something incorporeal (to which genus Xenocrates and his predecessors too had said the mind belonged) should be the agent of anything, and that only a body was capable of acting or of being acted upon" (SVF 1.90, translation: LS 45.A). The consequence of this reasoning is then that souls, moral virtues and qualities are all bodies, because they are capable of acting and being affected.[13] Indeed, if the soul were not a body, how could we account for its capacity of moving the body and for the visible interactions taking place between body and soul, for example when the body turns red or pale out of shame or fear? (SVF 1.518)

According to Brunschwig, the disjunction "acting *or* being acted upon" leaves open the possibility for some bodies to be only active or only passive.[14] This allows the Stoics to identify two ultimate principles of the whole reality, both of which are corporeal, but one of which is merely active (*to poioun*), that is, God or the *logos*, while the other is merely passive (*to paschon*), that is, matter (SVF 3.AnT.12). The active principle is also described as a self-moved power (*hē dunamis autokinētos*), an eternal principle of movement and the cause of the movement of unqualified matter, which, being entirely passive, is not capable of moving itself: "For this reason, as when we look at a very beautiful bronze we want to know the artist (since in itself the matter is in an immobile condition), so when we see the matter of the universe moving and possessing form and structure we might reasonably

13 Brunschwig (2003, 211).

14 Brunschwig (2003, 210).

inquire into the cause which moves and shapes it into many forms . . . So there exists a power which in itself is self-moving, and this must be divine and everlasting . . . But it will not be in motion from a definite time; for there will be no cause of its motion from a definite time. So, then, the power which moves matter and guides it in due order into generations and changes is everlasting. So this power would be god" (SVF 2.311, translation: LS 44.C).

While matter is passive and unqualified, the active principle is rational and creative: it is capable of transforming matter and itself, generating all the qualities that constitute the world. In contrast with the Platonic transcendence of the Forms and of intelligible reality, the Stoics held that the *logos* is immanent to the cosmos to which it gives life. It is by being present everywhere in the cosmos, permeating and pervading it, that the active principle encompasses the whole reality and keeps it together in a unified and cohesive living whole, which it directs and governs. Chrysippus defines this divine principle as the seminal reason of the cosmos, *spermatikos logos . . . tou kosmou*, which generates the four elements, previously existing in a state of indeterminacy as an unqualified substance (*apoio ousia*), that is, matter (SVF 2.580). The active principle, indeed, contains in itself the seminal reasons of everything and it is through them that it generates all beings, governs them and connects them all together (SVF 2.1027). The *spermatikoi logoi* are the principles of movement and change, and on the basis of them each event takes place in accordance with fate. In addition to being the cause of movement and change, seminal reasons are also the *dunameis* responsible for the self-identity and persistence of each individual substance; each being realizes itself according to its seminal reason (SVF 2.986).

The notion of *spermatikos logos* played an important role in the Middle Platonic elaboration on the efficacy of the Forms: these took on the productive and dynamic character of the Stoic *logoi* and came to be considered not only as paradigmatic, but also as efficient causes. Plotinus' notion of the forming principles (*logoi*), responsible for the existence of the whole of sensible reality and for its phenomena of change, is greatly indebted to the Stoic elaboration of the *dunamis* of the seminal reasons, although Plotinus strongly criticized the Stoic corporealist conception of *logoi*.

Potentiality and Actuality in Plotinus' Enneads

Platonic, Aristotelian and Stoic sources have all significantly influenced Plotinus' view on potentiality and actuality. However, it would be mistaken to think that Plotinus addresses these sources in a doxographic or eclectic fashion. On the contrary, the *Enneads* provide us with an original thought, where elements coming from the previous philosophical tradition are profoundly reworked and transformed in order to creatively birth a new coherent theoretical whole. Moreover, it should always be kept in mind that Plotinus viewed his philosophical work as an interpretation of Plato's dialogues, so that several aspects of his thought can be seen as attempts to solve the difficulties presented by Plato's writings. In particular, as we will see, Plotinus partially transforms the traditional Peripatetic conception of *dunamis* and *energeia* in such a manner as to offer an answer to the problem of the participation between Forms and sensible objects.

As many particular aspects of these notions of potentiality and actuality will be examined in detail in the commentary, it is useful here to give only a general overview. Let us start with the intelligible world. Plotinus attributes an active power (*dunamis*) to the intelligible realm taken as a whole.[15] Indeed, his notion of active power, influenced by the Stoic doctrine of the generative power of the *logos*, allows him to give an account of the efficient causality of intelligible realities, while at the same time denying that they are affected either by their own activity of generation or by the outcomes of their generative power. Moreover, each intelligible level transmits its generative power to the subsequent one in a process of generation that does not imply any deliberate plan or choice and that excludes

15 See for example: V.9 [5] 6, 9; 8, 8; V.4 [7] 2, 38; V.1 [10] 7, 9–10; V.3 [49] 15, 33–36.

any anthropomorphic account of creation. The capacity to generate is simply implied in the nature of each intelligible level, so that the emanation is a necessary process following from the very nature of the intelligible beings. While intelligible realities are active powers, Plotinus denies that we can attribute passive potentiality (*to dunamei*) to them, as this would render intelligible beings susceptible of being affected and therefore of undergoing change.[16]

The active power of intelligible realities can be seen, from another viewpoint, as their own *energeia* or inner activity. Intelligible beings are both in actuality and activities.[17] The intelligible realm is a living totality where each intelligible being is engaged in an activity of thought that constitutes its being.[18] Plotinus, indeed, considers life to be a form of activity. Being in actuality, intelligible realities are self-sufficient and perfect in their own being. Their inner activity, the act of their own self-constitution, moreover, is productive and has outcomes: by thinking themselves and their source, intelligible realities also generate the subsequent intelligible level, organized into a living ontological hierarchy.[19]

---

16 The active power of the One and its transmission to the subsequent intelligible levels will be discussed in greater detail in the *Commentary*.

17 See, for example: V.9 [5] 7, 6; V.9 [5] 10, 15; V.3 [49] 7.

18 See VI.7 [38] 12, 22–24; I.4 [46] 3, 33–40.

19 The notion of double *energeia* will be discussed in detail in the *Commentary*.

The case of the soul is more complex. Indeed, if we distinguish between three different levels of the soul, namely the hypostatic Soul, the soul of the world, and the individual soul, we can see how, while they are all active powers, their life and the actualization of this active power is different.[20] The hypostatic Soul, which is an activity,[21] is eternally contemplating the intelligible contents coming from Intellect and is always in possession of its thought-content, living a perfect life. These intelligible contents, the *logoi*, are activities themselves: they are the noetic contents of Intellect that the Soul receives in an ontologically weakened state.[22] The soul of the world projects these generative *logoi* upon matter, giving order and shape, and governing the cosmos: however, its activity is always the same, as the soul of the world is unaffected by the cosmos it governs and is eternally turned towards the higher Soul in an unchanging activity of contemplation.[23] The same does not hold for the individual soul once it detaches itself from the higher realm and descends into bodies. Indeed, while Plotinus insists that even in the case of the individual soul we cannot speak of passive potentiality, but must rather speak of its active power, he cannot deny that the individual soul's activities are not always the same. An

20 See IV.3 [27] 4.

21 See IV.4 [28] 16, 18.

22 See V.9 [5] 3 and 5; III.3 [48] 1, 4.

23 IV.3 [27] 4, 21–30.

individual soul can either fully realize its nature by turning itself toward Intellect or it can increasingly identify itself with the life in a body and forget its true self.[24] Moreover, it is evident that embodied individual souls go through processes of learning, as they are not always in contact with Intellect.

The generative power of the intelligible beings is transmitted from one level to another and then to sensible beings. In the sensible realm, everything is capable of generating and of having effects of any sort, because it participates in the active power coming from the intelligible realm through the *logoi* projected upon matter. However, the transmission of this generative power finds a limit in prime matter. Matter is entirely deprived of any capacity to generate, it is sterile, and is even incapable of turning itself toward its own source. While the intelligible reality is characterized by active power and by the absence of passive potentiality, we have with matter an inverted situation, as matter has no active power, it is nothing in actuality, and it is only in potentiality. It is, however, a passive potentiality of a peculiar kind, as Plotinus also holds that matter is impassible, that is, that it cannot be affected in any way and cannot be transformed.[25]

---

24 IV.8 [6] 4.

25 For the relevant references concerning matter and sensible objects, see the *Commentary* on chapters 4 and 5.

Finally, as we have said, phenomena of change in the sensible world must be explained through the active power of intelligible realities. Indeed, it is through the notion of *dunamis* that Plotinus explains how the soul can be present to sensible reality, have an efficient causality, and act upon bodies. This corresponds to a squarely anti-Aristotelian understanding of change, as the fundamental kind of causality playing a role in Plotinus' universe is vertical causality. Whether this excludes the presence of a genuine passive potentiality in the sensible world and of any kind of horizontal causality, however, is a controversial issue that will be addressed in more detail in the *Commentary*.

Ennead *II.5 [25]*

It is now time to turn to Plotinus' treatise *On What Is Potentially and What Actually*. This treatise is number 25 in the chronological list provided by Porphyry in his *Life of Plotinus*. On the basis of this chronology, in the treatises previously written, Plotinus had already largely resorted to notions of potentiality and actuality in order to describe the nature of being in the case of intelligible reality. The treatise appears then to be an attempt at clarification of his peculiar use of these notions and of the differences from Aristotle's own elaboration of the topic. Moreover, one can find many correspondences between treatise 25 and the following two treatises: III.6 [26] and IV.3 [27]. In the first of the two, Plotinus expands his elaboration of the nature of sensible objects and of matter, and many of the arguments against an Aristotelian hylomorphic conception of the sensible compounds can be better understood as a development of the arguments already articulated in II.5 about the peculiar way in which matter is said to be in potentiality. In IV.3, he has recourse, instead, to the notion of active power in order to explain the way the soul ensouls the world and individual bodies and is capable of exercising its own efficacity on them. Both treatises can be seen as rejecting Aristotle's view of hylomorphism, both concerning the constitution of sensible compounds, including artificial objects, and concerning the relation between soul and body.

Several aspects of Plotinus' view on potentiality and actuality are left out of II.5. Indeed, the aim of the treatise is to solve a few problems, listed at the very beginning of the text, and to clarify the differences from Aristotle's view on the topic: the outcome is a systematic account of the different meanings of potentiality and actuality and of the way each of these meanings applies or does not apply to the sensible realm, to the intelligible realm, and to matter. But this systematic account is not exhaustive, and several particular aspects of Plotinus' view of potentiality and actuality are not addressed: for example, we do not find here any explicit treatment either of the notion of power of everything or infinite power in reference to the One, or of the notion of double activity.

Plotinus' writing in this treatise is extremely dense and at times particularly dry in its technicality. The structure of the text unfolds in a coherent and cohesive manner, in spite of its difficulty, his habit of alternating dialogue, in which he answers a series of objections raised by an unnamed opponent, and long argumentative passages, in which he sometimes resorts to analogies and rhetorical devices, especially in order to describe the nature of matter. Chapter 1 begins with a series of three questions: i) What is the meaning of potential and actual being? ii) Are activity and actuality the same thing? iii) Does potential being apply to intelligible realities? These three questions are the guiding thread of the treatise. In the first two chapters Plotinus first mentions and then discusses some Peripatetic theses, without explicitly quoting his sources. In particular in chapter 2, he discusses them with reference to the embodied soul and to phenomena of changes in the sensible realm, where he introduces his notion of vertical causality, reaching a first systematic conclusion at the end of the chapter. This conclusion consists of a partial rectification of Aristotle's terminology. Indeed, Plotinus insists that we should carefully distinguish between *to dunamei* (passive potentiality or the capacity to be affected and acted upon) and *dunamis* (active power or the capacity to act upon and affect something else). Moreover, we should further distinguish *to energeiai* (being in actuality or actual being)—which is the compound of matter and form and must be said in relation to *to dunamei*—from, on the one hand, *energeia toude* (the immanent form of a compound), and, on the other, *energeia*, understood as activity and as the actual exercise of an active power.

In the rest of the treatise we will discover that this first conclusion, which holds in the case of sensible objects, applies only partially to the cases of intelligible reality and of prime matter, and should therefore be revised and integrated. The discussion of chapters 1–2, then, is preliminary to the treatment of potentiality and actuality in the intelligible realm in chapter 3, which Plotinus admittedly considers the core of the whole treatise. This treatment highlights the difference between sensible and intelligible reality, by arguing in favor of two main theses: that potential being (or passive potentiality), while applying to the sensible realm, does not apply to intelligible beings, and that in the case of intelligible reality being in actuality means by the same token being an activity, which is not the case for sensible objects. The last two chapters, finally, revise the conclusions reached in the preliminary discussion of chapters 1–2, showing how matter should be considered as a particular and unique case of potentiality without possibility of actualization: once again, this differentiates the case of matter from that of sensible objects.

Note on the Text

LINE NUMBERS IN THE TRANSLATION are approximate and do not always match the original Greek text. Since the commentary follows the sequence of the English translation, there may sometimes be a slight discrepancy in the ordering.

The Greek text adopted is that of the Oxford edition (taking into account the Addenda ad Textum in vol. 3, 304–325). Deviations from the text are noted in the commentary. Each *Ennead* is referred to by Roman numerals, followed by the number of the treatise, the chapter of the treatise, and, finally, separated by a comma, the line number or numbers, e.g, V.1.3, 24–27.

It is customary to add the chronological number given by Porphyry in his *Life of Plotinus* (*Vita Plotini*), so that, for example, V.1 is designated V.1 [10]. In this series the chronological number is given only where it is of significance for Plotinus' philosophical stance. The following chart indicates the chronological order.

Chronological Order of the ***Enneads***

Enn.		*Enn.*		*Enn.*		*Enn.*		*Enn.*		*Enn.*	
I.1	**53**	II.1	**40**	III.1	**3**	IV.1	**21**	V.1	**10**	VI.1	**42**
I.2	**19**	II.2	**14**	III.2	**47**	IV.2	**4**	V.2	**11**	VI.2	**43**
I.3	**20**	II.3	**52**	III.3	**48**	IV.3	**27**	V.3	**49**	VI.3	**44**
I.4	**46**	II.4	**12**	III.4	**15**	IV.4	**28**	V.4	**7**	VI.4	**22**
I.5	**36**	II.5	**25**	III.5	**50**	IV.5	**29**	V.5	**32**	VI.5	**23**
I.6	**1**	II.6	**17**	III.6	**26**	IV.6	**41**	V.6	**24**	VI.6	**34**
I.7	**54**	II.7	**37**	III.7	**45**	IV.7	**2**	V.7	**18**	VI.7	**38**
I.8	**51**	II.8	**35**	III.8	**30**	IV.8	**6**	V.8	**31**	VI.8	**39**
I.9	**16**	II.9	**33**	III.9	**13**	IV.9	**8**	V.9	**5**	VI.9	**9**

	Enn.		*Enn.*		*Enn.*		*Enn.*		*Enn.*		*Enn.*
1	I.6	**10**	V.1	**19**	I.2	**28**	IV.4	**37**	II.7	**46**	I.4
2	IV.7	**11**	V.2	**20**	I.3	**29**	IV.5	**38**	VI.7	**47**	III.2
3	III.1	**12**	II.4	**21**	IV.1	**30**	III.8	**39**	VI.8	**48**	III.3
4	IV.2	**13**	III.9	**22**	VI.4	**31**	V.8	**40**	II.1	**49**	V.3
5	V.9	**14**	II.2	**23**	VI.5	**32**	V.5	**41**	IV.6	**50**	III.5
6	IV.8	**15**	III.4	**24**	V.6	**33**	II.9	**42**	VI.1	**51**	I.8
7	V.4	**16**	I.9	**25**	II.5	**34**	VI.6	**43**	VI.2	**52**	II.3
8	IV.9	**17**	II.6	**26**	III.6	**35**	II.8	**44**	VI.3	**53**	I.1
9	VI.9	**18**	V.7	**27**	IV.3	**36**	I.5	**45**	III.7	**54**	I.7

Synopsis

Chapter 1

1–10 Three questions:

(i) What is potential and actual being?

(ii) Is actual being identical to activity?

(iii) Is there potential being among intelligible realities?

10–21 Exposition of three main features of being in potentiality according to the Aristotelian tradition:

Something is always potentially a determinate kind of thing.

Something is potential if it can be transformed while either a) remaining or b) being destroyed through the process of change.

(i) A potential being, though it is potential with regard to the actual being it can become, is already something else in actuality.

21–29 Distinction between potential being and active power. Potential being corresponds to actual being, while power corresponds to activity.

29–34 Identification between potential being and passive potentiality: potential being is a substrate for affections, shapes, and forms.

Chapter 2

1–15 Question: Do potential beings become in actuality when they receive a form and remain themselves?

Answer: When a new, different being comes to be, we cannot say that a potential thing becomes actual. On the contrary, from a previous thing in potentiality a second thing in actuality comes to be.

15–26 Question: When a potentially learned man becomes an actual learned man, are what is potential and what is actual the same?

Answer: In this case the potential being is not the unlearned man, but the soul, as it had in itself a convenient predisposition.

26–36 *Energeia* has two meanings:

(i) It is the form (*eidos*) of a determinate thing.

(ii) It is the exercise of an active power.

Chapter 3

1–4 Four questions:

(i) In which sense does actual being apply to intelligible realities?

(ii) Is each of the intelligible realities only in actuality or also activity?

(iii) Are intelligible realities as a whole activity?

(iv) Is there potential being among intelligible realities?

4–22 Answer to question (iv): There is no potential being among intelligible realities, because there is no time and possibility of change. Two possible objections: intelligible matter and the individual soul are in potentiality. Answer: intelligible matter is a form and the soul is an active power.

22–40 Answer to questions (i), (ii) and (iii): intelligible realities are both in actuality, as they are perfect and self-sufficient, and activities. They are eternal life.

Chapter 4

1–6 Question: Is prime matter an actual being? Answer: Matter is not something in actuality, because it is everything in potentiality.

6–18 Matter is non-being: it is neither a Form nor a sensible being in actuality.

Chapter 5

1–10 Matter is nothing in actuality and is everything in potentiality. If matter were something in actuality, it would not be prime matter, but rather proximate matter.

10–23 Matter is unable to transform itself. Imprisoned between two kinds of being, intelligible and sensible, matter does not succeed in becoming either in actuality.

23–36 Matter is a "phantasm in actuality," a "lie in actuality," a "true lie," a "real non-being." Critique of hylomorphism.

Translation of
Plotinus Ennead *II.5 [25]*

1. There is said to be potential being, on the one hand, and actual being, on the other. But there is also something said to be activity among the beings. Therefore it is necessary to investigate what potential being is and what actual being.

Is activity the same as actual being? In other words, if something is actual being then is it also activity? Or rather is one different from the other so that what is actual need not | also be activity?

Now, while it is evident that among sensible realities there is potential being, we need to inquire whether this is also found among intelligible realities. Rather it is the case that only actual being can be found there. For even if there is potential being there, it always remains only potential, and even if it existed eternally, it would never become actual, for it would be hindered by the absence of time.

| But first we need to say what potential being is, if it is true that potential being cannot be said in an unqualified manner: for it is not possible that a potential being is potentially nothing. For example, the bronze is potentially a statue. Indeed if nothing came out of it or upon it, if it were not about to be something else after what it already was and if it did not have the possibility of becoming, then it would be only what it already was. But what it was, was already present and was not about to be. What else, then, | did it have the potentiality to be, after what was already present? Therefore it would not be potential at all. Moreover, a potential being must be called "potential," while already being something else in actuality, in virtue of being able to become also something else after what it already was, either by remaining along with the production of that thing, or yielding itself to the thing that it is able to become, and so perishing. | For "bronze is potentially a statue" in one manner, while water is potentially bronze and air is potentially fire in another.

If potential being is this sort of thing, is it the case that we should call it also a "power" in relation to what is about to be? For example, should we say that bronze is the power of the statue?

It depends. If power is taken to be active power, then this is certainly not the case. For, if power is understood as active power, it cannot be said to be potential. | However, if "potential being" is said not only in relation to actual being, but also in relation to activity, then power is also in potentiality. But it is better and clearer to say that potential being refers to actual being, while power refers to activity. | So then, a potential being such as this is like a substrate for the affections, shapes, and forms that it is about to receive and is naturally predisposed toward. Moreover, potential beings strive to reach them, and some are directed toward improvement, while others are directed toward detriment and destruction, and each of them is also something else in actuality.

2. Concerning matter we need to investigate whether it is by being something else in actuality that matter is potential with regard to what is formed, or whether it is by not being in actuality at all. And in general, we also need to investigate whether the other things that we call potential become actual when they receive a form and remain themselves, or whether "actual being" should be predicated of the statue only insofar as we oppose | the actual statue to the potential statue but should not be predicated of the thing which we call "potential statue." If this is the case, a potential being does not become actual, but rather from a previous thing in potentiality a subsequent thing in actuality comes to be. And indeed, once again, the actual being | is the compound, not matter, on the one hand, and the form that is upon matter, on the other. And this is the case if another substance comes to

be, as in the example of the bronze statue: for the statue, *qua* compound, is a different substance. And in the case of things that do not remain at all, it is evident that the potential being was a completely different thing.

On the contrary, when a potentially learned man | becomes an actually learned man, in this case how could what is potential and what is actual not be the same? For, it is the same Socrates who is wise in potentiality and in actuality. Then, does this mean that the ignorant man and the man of knowledge are the same? For, the ignorant man was a man of knowledge in potentiality.

Rather, the unlearned man is a man of knowledge by accident. Indeed, he was not potentially a man of knowledge in virtue of the fact of being unlearned. On | the contrary, for him being unlearned was by accident, while the potential being was the soul, as it had in itself a convenient predisposition, in virtue of which he actually became a man of knowledge.

Yet, does he preserve his potential being then, and does he remain a potentially learned man once he is learned in actuality?

There are no obstacles to this if we understand it in this other way: while earlier he was only in potentiality, now potentiality is in possession of | its form.

If therefore the potential being is the substrate, the actual being is the compound, that is, the statue, what should one call the form that is upon the bronze?

It is not absurd to call the shape and the form the "activity" in virtue of which the statue is in actuality and not only in potentiality: not "activity" in general, but the activity of | that determinate thing. Since it would be perhaps more appropriate to call "activity" the other one too, namely the activity that is in opposition to the power that brings it about. For the potential being receives its actual being from something else, whereas in the case of power activity is that which it is capable of by itself: for example, a disposition and the activity named according to it, like courage and behaving courageously. | Enough on this, then.

3. Now it is time to deal with the question for the sake of which these things have been said by way of preface, namely: in what sense do we speak of actual being among the intelligible realities? Is each of them only in actuality or activity as well? Taken together as a whole, are they activity? And is there potential being there?

If, indeed, there is no matter there, in which there could be potential being, and if none | of the intelligible realities is about to be something that it is not already, and if nothing gives birth to something else, either changing into something else or remaining what it is, and nothing gives being to something else in its place by giving itself up, then there is nothing there where there could be potential being, even more so as the [intelligible] realities are eternal and not in time.

Hence, if someone were to ask those who posit matter there, among the intelligible realities, | is there not potential being there, corresponding to the matter that is there—for even if matter is there in another way, nonetheless in each [intelligible] reality there will be something like matter, something like form, as well as the compound of the two—what will we answer?

What is there in the way of matter is a form, since even the soul, which is a form, can be matter in respect to something else.

Then, will it [intelligible matter] also be in potentiality with respect to that something else?

It will not. For we did say that that something else is its form, and yet | this form does not arrive later and, moreover, is not separated except conceptually, and it is in this way that [the intelligible reality] has matter as well, in the sense that it is conceived of as divided into two parts, whereas both [matter and form] are of the same nature. For example, Aristotle says that quintessence is immaterial.

But concerning the soul, what shall we answer? For it is a living being in potentiality, | when it is not a living being yet but is about to be, and is musical in potentiality and all those things that it becomes, not being them at all times: in this way there would be potential being among the intelligible realities as well.

This is not the case, because the soul is not these things in potentiality, but it is rather the power of these things.

But, concerning actual being, how is it there? Is it in the way the statue is the compound in actuality, because each of them [the intelligible realities] has received the form?

No, it is rather because each of them is a form and is perfectly what it is. Intellect, indeed, does not go from the capacity of thinking | to the act of thinking—for in this case it would be in need of another intellect, prior to it and that does not go from potentiality to actuality. On the contrary, the whole is within it. Indeed, in order to become something in actuality, a potential being demands to be brought into actuality by something else coming to it, while that which has itself from itself its being always in such a way, this is activity. | Therefore, all the first principles are activity: because it is from themselves and eternally that they have what they need to have. To be sure, the Soul is this way as well, not the soul that is in matter, but the Soul in the intelligible. But the soul that is in matter is also another activity—for example, the vegetative soul. For even this is an activity, as to what it is.

But if all realities are in actuality and are this way, then are they all activity? And | how?

Well, if it is beautifully said that that nature is sleepless, and is life, and is perfect life, then the most beautiful activities will be there. All [intelligible] realities, then, are both in actuality and activity, and all are lives, and the region there is the region of life, and the origin and source of true soul and intellect. |

4. Therefore, all other beings that are potentially something are also another thing in actuality, which, while being in actuality, is said to be potential in relation to something else. But concerning matter, which is said to exist, and which we say is potentially everything, how then would it be possible to say that it is one of the beings in actuality? For in this case it would not be potentially | everything. If therefore matter is none of the beings, it will necessarily be non-being. Indeed, how could it be something in actuality, if it is none of the beings?

But even if it is none of those beings that are generated upon it, nothing prevents it from being something else, if it is true that not all beings are generated upon matter.

Now, insofar as matter is none of the things generated | upon it, and these are beings, matter is non-being. Certainly it is not a form either, since it is imagined as formless: hence it cannot be counted among the intelligibles either. Therefore in this sense too it will be non-being. As it is non-being on both accounts, so it is non-being to a higher degree. If, then, it has fled the nature of the beings that truly are, and | it cannot attain to those that are falsely said to be, for it is not even an image of a rational principle the way those are, in what kind of being could it be grasped? And if it cannot be grasped in any kind of being, what kind of thing could it be in actuality?

5. How, then, shall we speak of it? And how is it the matter of the existent things?

Insofar as it is in potentiality.

So then, insofar as it is already in potentiality, is it therefore already in accordance with what is going to be?

But being for it is only a promise of what is going to be: as if its being were deferred to what is going to be. Moreover, it is not *some* thing in potentiality, but rather *every* thing in potentiality: | and since it is nothing in itself, except what it is, namely matter, it is not in actuality either. For if it were something in actuality, it would be that actual being, and not matter: therefore, it would not be matter in every way, but rather in the way that bronze is matter. Matter is therefore this—non-being—but not as "different from being" the way movement is. For movement too is carried upon being, as if it were from | and in being. Matter, instead, is like a reject, entirely separated, and incapable of transforming itself, as it rather always remains the way it was from the beginning: namely, non-being. It was neither something in actuality from the beginning, for it was apart from all beings, nor did it become anything in actuality: it did not even have the capacity of getting some color | from those things that wanted to descend into it. On the contrary, remaining directed toward something else, for it is potentially with respect to what comes after it, appearing once the intelligible beings have left off, and being caught by the things that are generated after it, it takes the last place among them. Therefore, being caught by both, it is neither of them in actuality, | but it is left to be only potentially a kind of weak and faint phantasm, incapable of being shaped. So, it is a phantasm in actuality. So, it is a lie in actuality.

This is the same as being a "true lie." This is the same as being "real non-being." If, therefore, it is non-being in actuality, it is non-being to an higher degree, hence real non-being. It is necessary, then, | that what has its truth in non-being is far removed from being something in actuality. So, if it is necessary for it to be, it is necessary for it to be non-being in actuality, so that, having departed from true being, it may have its being in non-being. For, in the case of false beings, if you take away their falsity, you take away the only substance they had, | and if you bring to actuality those things that have their being and substance in potentiality, you destroy the cause of their existence, for their being consists of potentiality. If then it is necessary to keep matter as indestructible, it is necessary to keep it as matter. So, as it seems, it is necessary to say that it is only in potentiality, so that it may be what it is, | or else one must refute these arguments.

Commentary

Chapter 1

In this chapter Plotinus outlines the issues that he will discuss in the rest of this short, but rather dense, treatise. He begins with three questions: i) What are potential and actual being? ii) Are actual being and activity identical? iii) Is there a potential being among the intelligible realities? He then focuses on the nature of potential being and provides a concise summary of some Aristotelian theses concerning dunamis (potentiality)*—the sources of which might be* Metaphysics 9, Physics *3, and* On the Soul (De Anima) *2. Finally, he draws a first distinction between passive potentiality, or potential being, and active power, and concludes by defining potential being as the substrate of affections, shapes, and forms.*

1, 1–10 The first lines of the treatise introduce some of the technical terminology that Plotinus will reserve to indicate specific forms of potentiality and actuality. *To dunamei* and *to energeiai* (the article *to* in the nominative combined with the nouns *dunamei* and *energeiai* in the dative) refer to potential and actual being, respectively, while the nominative *energeia* corresponds to activity. As we will discover in the second part of this chapter (lines 23–28), potential being (*to dunamei*) is to be understood as passive potentiality, that is, the capacity to be acted upon and to suffer a change of some sort. For the clarification of the distinction between activity (*energeia*) and actual being (*to energeiai*) in the sensible realm we will need to wait until the end of chapter 2, where we will discover that actual being corresponds to the compound of matter and form, and therefore to the actualization of a potential being. On the contrary, activity is the realization of an active power (*dunamis*): for example, my seeing an object, which is an activity, is the actualization of my active capacity to see. This definition and distinction do not apply to intelligible realities, which are in actuality not because they are the realization of a potential being, but rather because they are eternally self-identical and self-sufficient. This point will be elaborated on in chapter 3.

As already mentioned, in the initial lines of this chapter, Plotinus raises a series of three questions concerning i) the nature of actual and potential being, ii) the difference or identity between actual being and activity, and iii) the kind of *dunamis* that can be ascribed to the intelligible realm. Only the third question is immediately addressed, while the first two remain unanswered at this stage. Plotinus suggests that the absence of time in the intelligible realm excludes the presence of passive potentiality among the intelligibles; however, this answer is only provisional, as Plotinus will further elaborate this point in chapter 3.

1, 1 *There is said . . . on the other*: The *legetai* that opens the treatise indicates that the notions of potentiality and actuality were common themes of inquiry and discussion in philosophical circles. *Legetai* (*there is said to be*) at line 1 and *skepteon* (*it is necessary to investigate*) at line 2 build a nice contrast. We commonly employ these terms and notions in our conversations, or, these terms and notions are widespread in philosophical environments: this is why it is necessary to investigate further, and to consider the correct way to employ them.

1, 4 *in other words . . . it also activity*: For this sentence I follow the *Addenda and Corrigenda* of HS_1: *ei ti estin energeiai, touto kai energeia*: "is what is in actuality also activity?" In HS_1 and HS_2 the Greek reads: *ei ti estin energeia, touto kai energeiai*, which might be translated as "whether what is activity is also in actuality." As is shown by the following two lines (5–6), the problem Plotinus is addressing is not whether an activity is also something in actuality, but whether from the existence of a being in actuality, say a chair or a bronze statue, we must conclude that this being is an activity as well. In other words, is the actual being that belongs to a chair, and in virtue of which the chair exists and is this determinate kind of being, simultaneously also an activity? An analogous question is raised in 3, 34–35 in relation to intelligible realities, which are said to be in actuality because they are eternally what they are: "But if all realities are in actuality and are in this way, then are they all activity?" (*all'energeiai men panta kai houtōs, energeia de panta*). The text suggested by the *Addenda and Corrigenda* to HS_1 enables us to understand line 4 as raising precisely this question. See also Narbonne (1998, 39).

1, 6–7 *Now, while it . . . among intelligible realities*: Plotinus seems to consider it uncontroversial that one can speak of potential being, or passive potentiality, in the case of sensible realities. Indeed, for Aristotle passive potentiality—the capacity of being affected and being acted upon by an agent—is a key notion for the explanation of change. While within an Aristotelian framework it is evident that there is potential being among sensible realities, it is less so in Plotinus' account of sensible reality, and some scholars have argued that in Plotinus' view of the sensible world there is no room for passive potentiality as the potency to be affected. See Emilsson (1998, 126–127) and Pigler (2008, 506–507). Hence we have two possible interpretations of these lines: either Plotinus accepts some form of passive potentiality among sensible beings and therefore is sincere when he says that this does not require any demonstration, or he believes that passive potentiality does not play any role in phenomena of change and therefore he is just postponing the moment of the refutation of the Aristotelian view on this subject.

1, 9 *For even if... never become actual*: The argument of this line is relatively simple. In the intelligible realm there is no time: intelligible beings are eternal, they are not generated in time, they cannot be corrupted and they cannot be destroyed. But time, according to Aristotle, is necessary for movement and change. Indeed, in *Physics* 4.12.220b–221a, Aristotle defines time as the measure of movement and stresses that, for movement, being in time means being measured through time. If it is true that among the intelligible realities there is no time, then admitting that intelligible beings are in potentiality will force us to say that they cannot be brought to actuality. Indeed, the passage from being in potentiality to being in actuality requires time. So, if we admit that an intelligible being is potential in the way bronze is in relation to the statue, we are then compelled to maintain that it will eternally remain potential. This is problematic, as it would imply that intelligible beings are characterized by lack and imperfection, which is absurd because perfection is a necessary feature of the intelligible realm.

1, 9–10 *for it would . . . the absence of time*: The manuscripts read *ou tō chronō exeirgesthai*, and this passage has received several different emendations. Theiler's emendation, <*tōi*> *ou tōi chronōi*, has been accepted by Armstrong, who translates: "it is excluded from it by the fact that it is not in time." Henry and Schwyzer made various proposals: HS$_1$ suggested *tōi ou chronōi*, HS$_2$ suggested *ou tōi chronōi*, HS$_4$ accepted Igal's suggestion to emend the text as *houtō* <*tōi*> *chronōi*. This last proposal is based on a passage in Aristotle's *Categories* 13a30–31 that deals with the issue of change from contrary to contrary. A vicious man can progress toward virtue, unless he is prevented from doing so by time (*chronōi exeirgētai*), in the sense of "by the absence of time." Narbonne accepts Igal's reference to the *Categories* but insists that in this case the negation *ou* is superfluous and that Igal's suggestion to read *houtō* is problematic because it is unclear what *houtō* would refer to. He therefore follows Kirchhoff and deletes *ou*: *[ou] tōi chronōi exeirgesthai*. My translation follows Kirchhoff's and Narbonne's reading.

1, 10–21 Here and elsewhere in the *Commentary* I draw largely on Arruzza (2011).

Here we find the exposition of a series of Aristotelian theses concerning potential and actual being. In this exposition Plotinus is not yet taking a position, and we will need to read the rest of the treatise to understand which of the theses he supports and which he criticizes or at least significantly transforms. The intent and nature of this exposition, however, is not properly doxographic, as Plotinus is interested not so much in reporting about the Aristotelian tradition, but rather in theoretically discussing, appropriating in an original way, transforming or straightforwardly rejecting only those aspects of the Aristotelian conception of *dunamis* and *energeia* that are relevant to his own theoretical purposes.

Three main features of being in potentiality according to the Aristotelian tradition are set out. First, something is always potentially a determinate kind of thing (or a certain number of things in the case of artificial objects), as it is not possible to say that something is a potential being in the abstract or that it is a bare potentiality, without reference to a corresponding particular thing it could actually (*energeiai*) become. See Aristotle, *Metaphysics* 9.5.1047b35–1048a2. In 1048a15–20, Aristotle specifies, with respect to the rational potencies, that potentiality cannot be understood in an absolute sense: a number of particular conditions—such as, for instance, the absence of internal and external impediments—must be satisfied, in order to say that something is potentially something else: "And it has the potentiality in question when the passive object is present and is in a certain state; if not it will not be able to act. To add the qualification 'if nothing external prevents' is not further necessary; for it has the potentiality in so far as this is a potentiality of acting, and it is this not in all circumstances but on certain conditions, among which will be the exclusion of external hindrances; for these are barred by some of the positive qualifications" (translation: Ross, revised by Barnes). See also 1049aff. and *On Interpretation* (*De Interpretatione*) 22b36–23a26.

Second, something is potential if it can be transformed while either a) remaining or b) being destroyed through the process of change.

Third, a potential being, though it is potential with regard to the actual being it can become, is already something else in actuality, that is, it is already a determinate compound of form and matter. For instance, a piece of wood is potential if considered in relation to the table it might eventually become, but in itself, as a piece of wood, it is already a determinate thing (*tode ti*) in actuality. Moreover, according to Aristotle, not only can we distinguish for each compound a formal cause, which is in actuality, from a matter, which is in potentiality, but each compound has efficient causes that are in actuality. In the case of natural beings, the efficient cause is of the same species of the thing produced: man, for example, begets man. See *Metaphysics* 9.8.1049b4–29; 12.5.1071a6–11.

1, 10 *But first we . . . potential being is*: Plotinus seems to correct himself and to establish a more rigorous program for the inquiry. In order to examine whether there is potential being (*to dunamei*) among intelligible beings, it is necessary to first establish more precisely what potential being is. Indeed, the analysis of *to dunamei* will be the focus of the rest of chapter 1 and the whole of chapter 2, and only after having articulated this analysis will Plotinus deal with intelligible beings again, in chapter 3.

1, 10–11 *if it is . . . an unqualified manner*: A potential being is such only if it is potentiality of something and if it is so in a qualified manner, or—as Aristotle specifies in *Metaphysics* 9.5.1048a—it is potentially something determinate, in a determinate time, and in a determinate manner. Natural objects, such as seeds, are potential beings only in relation to the kind of full grown plants or animals of which they are a privation. For example, the seed of an apple tree is a privation of an apple tree and is therefore potentially only this kind of tree and not an oak. Artificial objects, on the contrary, are potentially a set of determinate things (see Natali 2008). In these lines, Plotinus refers to the traditional example of bronze and the statue: it is not that bronze is potentiality of nothing or is potential in general, but rather it is potential in relation to the statue that the bronze will become after having received a determinate shape. But bronze might be said to be potentially other things as well, for example a door: we must then suppose that there is a finite set of objects that the bronze is capable of becoming. The set of things that a natural object can artificially become is limited by the specific nature of the object, which sets some determinate boundaries to the kind of technical transformations that the object can undergo. Wool, for example, can receive the shape of a saw but it will never be a real one, because it cannot fulfil the function of a saw, namely to cut. Thus to claim that wool is potentially a saw is incorrect.

This passage, until line 16, is quoted by Simplicius in *Commentary on the Physics* (*In physicorum*) 3.1.399.2–6. Here, Simplicius comments on *Physics* 3.1.200b26, where Aristotle claims that among the beings, there is i) something that is only in actuality, and ii) something that is both in actuality and in potentiality. Simplicius takes i) to refer to ungenerated beings and to primary forms without matter, while ii) refers to generated beings which are compounds of form and matter. Simplicius partially corrects Aristotle, observing that a more complete distinction would be one that differentiates among i) things that are only in actuality, ii) things that are both in potentiality and in actuality, iii) and things that are only in potentiality. Indeed, after quoting Plotinus' passage until "after what was already present," Simplicius asks the question: "What would be only in potentiality, then?" (3.1.399.6–7), and he finds the answer in the conclusive part of Plotinus' treatise, where prime matter is addressed: prime matter is only in potentiality. Simplicius, however, is careful in stressing that this is the case, because prime matter is non-being.

1, 12–13 *the bronze is potentially a statue*: The bronze and the statue is a classic Aristotelian example for passive potentiality. See *Physics* 3.1.201a30.

1, 17 *a potential being . . . else in actuality*: This passage is controversial, as it can be plausibly translated in different ways. The Greek text (*ti on allo ēdē*) literally reads: "being already something else." Armstrong translated *ti on allo ēdē* as "already potentially something else." This translation is unconvincing because it transforms this sentence into either a mere tautology of the kind "something is called potential because it is already potential," or a mere repetition of the previous argument: "something is called potential because it is already potentially *something else*," namely, it is the potency of a determinate being, and is not potential in absolute terms. Moreover, if we follow Armstrong's translation, it becomes difficult to understand why Plotinus writes *ēdē*, "already." This "already" is, in fact, very important: it indicates what Plotinus really means, namely that something that is potential in relation to something else, is *already* a being of some kind—it is already something else in actuality. This is the translation suggested by Narbonne. Narbonne's version is both grammatically plausible (if we consider *ti on allo ēdē*, "being already something else," as a circumstantial participle referring to *to dunamei*) and conceptually justified with regard to the purpose of lines 10–21. Plotinus is exposing the main features of potential being and its relation to actual being in Aristotelian thought. Among those features is the fact that what is potential from one point of view is, from another point of view, some other thing in actuality. Water, for example, can be considered both as an individual actual substance, water, and as ice in potentiality. Furthermore, this interpretation allows us to understand why Plotinus discusses this argument again at the beginning of chapter 4 with reference to prime matter.

This passage, until line 21, is quoted by Simplicius, *Commentary on the Physics* (*In physicorum*), 3.1.398.33–399.1. Simplicius patchworks Plotinus' passages, as he quotes lines 17–21 immediately before lines 10–16. See the commentary above: 1.10–11.

1, 17–20 *in virtue of . . . was and so perishing*: These lines can be understood in two different ways, on the basis of the Aristotelian account of the different kinds of change (see, for example, *Metaphysics* 8.1.1042a32–b8 where Aristotle distinguishes between local motion, growth, alteration, and substantial change). In *Metaphysics* 9.7.1049a29–39, Aristotle says that we can distinguish two different kinds of substrate of change. In one case, the substrate of change plays the role of a *tode ti*, that is, of a determinate being that accounts for the substrate of accidental attributes and, therefore, remains throughout and after the change: the man becomes musical and this change is expressed by the adjective "musical" that is predicated of the substance "man." In the second case, the substrate does not play the role of a *tode ti* within the process of change, but rather of matter, which is indeterminate in contrast to the form that is predicated of it. In this case the predicate is a form, and the substrate remains only as the matter of the substance produced through the process of change. For example, the piece of wood that receives the shape of a casket becomes the proximate matter of the casket and remains in the new *tode ti*— "casket"—as its matter and its potential being, or privation. This is why we call the outcome of this change a "wooden casket": "For the subject and substratum differ by being or not being a 'this'; the substratum of *accidents* is an individual such as a man, i.e. body and soul, while the accident is something like musical or white. (The subject is called, when music is implanted in it, not music but musical, and the man is not whiteness but white, and not ambulation or movement but walking or moving,—as in the above examples of 'of' something. Wherever this is so, then, the ultimate subject is a substance; but when this is not so but the predicate is a form or a 'this,' the ultimate subject is matter and material substance" (1049a27–36, translation: Ross, revised by Barnes).

The change that takes place when the subject is a substance can be called qualitative change, or alteration. The change that takes place when the subject is matter or a material substance can be called substantial change, or generation, because the outcome of the process of change is a new *this*, a *tode ti*, which did not exist before and that comes to be because of the process of change suffered by the wood. Substantial change can be of two kinds as well, for sometimes the previous substance is entirely destroyed in the process of change, for example when wood is burned and becomes ashes, whereas sometimes the previous substance remains in the new *tode ti*, but only *qua* matter. Bronze or marble, for example, becomes the matter of the new statue that came to be, and are not entirely destroyed in the process of change. In *On Generation and Corruption* (*De generatione et corruptione*) 1.4.319b, Aristotle states that a change is qualitative and not substantial when 1) there is a perceptible substrate that remains, 2) the affections that are altered are those of the subject itself, and 3) the affections directly refer to and are properties of the substrate that remains.

In light of these considerations, and taking into account that the context of this chapter is the discussion of Aristotelian theses concerning potentiality and actuality, a first possible interpretation of lines 17–20 is that here Plotinus refers to the Aristotelian distinction between qualitative and substantial change: something is said to be in potentiality, with regard to its capacity either of suffering an alteration or of becoming a new substance. A second possible interpretation is that Plotinus is referring more specifically to the distinction between two different kinds of substantial change in the Aristotelian tradition: something is called potential with regard to its capacity of becoming a new substance, either remaining in the new substance as its matter, or being entirely destroyed during the process of change. In order to solve this puzzle we need to examine the following two lines, where Plotinus resorts to some examples.

The use of the Aristotelian terminology of substantial and qualitative change needs to be read with some caution, for it can be understood only improperly in a Plotinian context. For Plotinus sensible objects do not count as proper substances; only intelligible realities can be considered substances. Nevertheless it is still possible for Plotinus to distinguish different kinds of change. Indeed, Plotinus speaks of changes in which the outcome is a new being, that is, *something else*.

1, 20 *For "bronze . . . in one manner*: In the previous lines Plotinus asserted that something is called potential "in virtue of being able to become something other than itself, either by remaining along with the production of that thing, or giving itself over to the thing that it is able to become, and so perishing." The examples of the bronze becoming a statue, water becoming bronze, and air becoming fire, need to be taken as illustrations of this point. If the previous lines are about the distinction between qualitative and substantial change, then we should take the bronze becoming a statue as an example of qualitative change, while the transformation of water into bronze and air into fire are examples of substantial change. Within an Aristotelian framework, however, this would appear problematic. According to Aristotle, the transformation of bronze into a statue is a change of shape or *schēmatisis*. In *Physics* 7.246a1–4, Aristotle clearly distinguishes the change of shape from qualitative change: "Since, therefore, having regard to the figure or shape of a thing we no longer call that which has become of a certain figure by the name of the material that exhibits the figure, whereas having regard to a thing's affections or alterations we still call it by the name of its material, it is evident that becomings of the former kind cannot be alterations" (translation: Hardie-Gaye 1930). One may say that bronze becomes hot or cold or that it can be colored in a certain way, giving to the matter a qualitative (adjectival) attribute, which derives from the name of the kind of alteration it underwent: cold bronze, red bronze, and so on. On the contrary, when bronze receives a shape, the name of the shaped bronze is not derived from the material substrate, but rather from the shape which is added to it in the process of change. In other words, if bronze receives the shape of a statue, the outcome of the change will not be called "statuary bronze," but a "bronze statue." On the basis of this linguistic habit, we can conclude that the *schēmatisis* that takes place in the transformation of the bronze into a statue is not an alteration but a particular kind of generation (*genesis*). Moreover, keeping in mind the specifications of *On Generation and Corruption* 1.4.319b mentioned above, if the statue that comes to be is not an inherent property of the bronze from which it comes to be, then the permanence of a perceptible substrate is not sufficient for us to consider the transfiguration of bronze as a qualitative change. It will therefore be a substantial change. Of course, this is a kind of substantial change that implies the permanence of the perceptible material substrate, and not the complete destruction of the previous substance. However, even though we must say that the substrate remains in cases of *schēmatisis* like the one we have just analyzed, we have to add that it remains only as the matter of the new substance produced through the change. See also *Physics* 1.7.190b, where the change of shape (with the classic example of the bronze and the statue) is listed as one of the ways in which a substance is generated from a substrate.

This leads us back to the interpretation of lines 17–20. Here Plotinus is not distinguishing between alteration and substantial change in Aristotelian terms, but rather between two different kinds of substantial change, or of changes in which a new thing comes to be. The first, exemplified by the bronze and the statue, is that in which the previous object is not entirely destroyed in the process of change, but remains as the matter of the new object. The second is that in which the previous object perishes in the process of change, as in the case of the transformation of an element into a determinate material (water becoming bronze) or of an element into another (air becoming fire). This means that Plotinus is not examining examples of qualitative change, where no new object comes to be, at this stage.

For an alternative reading of 1, 17–21, see Narbonne (1998, 26 and 79). Narbonne suggests that Plotinus introduces here the distinction between qualitative and substantial change, as belonging to Aristotle and the Aristotelian tradition. To be sure, Plotinus will reject this distinction later, on the basis of his non-hylomorphic conception of sensible beings as aggregates of qualities. Indeed, in Narbonne's view, every change has an absolute character for Plotinus.

1, 21 *while water is potentially bronze*: the idea that bronze is derived from water is probably based on Plato, *Timaeus* 59b–c. See also Aristotle, *Metaphysics* 5.4.1015a8–10 and 5.24.1023a28–29.

1, 21–29 Plotinus concludes his summary of Aristotelian views on *dunamis* and *energeia* at line 21. The argument then proceeds with a distinction already introduced by Aristotle, but which, presumably, Plotinus considers insufficiently developed: the distinction between passive potentiality and active power, on the one hand, and between being in actuality and activity, on the other. To be sure, Aristotle stresses the dual meaning of *dunamis*, as passive potentiality and as the capacity to act in *Metaphysics* 5.12.1019a15ff.

and 9.1.1046a9ff. He specifies that we can speak of *dunamis* in two senses, either as the capacity to be acted upon—for example, the capacity of a patient to be healed—or as the capacity to act—for example, the capacity to walk or to speak—but Aristotle does not provide a distinct terminology for the two different meanings. Contrary to Aristotle, Plotinus introduces a clear terminological distinction in order to mark and to sharply distinguish these two aspects, active and passive, of *dunamis*. On the basis of his rigorous distinction of the different terms, Plotinus then establishes a direct correspondence, on the one hand, between potential being (*to dunamei*) and actual being (*to energeiai*), and, on the other, between active power (*dunamis*) and activity (*energeia*). This terminological distinction, as it will appear more clearly later, is the prelude to Plotinus' radical exclusion of potential being, that is, passive potentiality, from the intelligible realm.

1, 21 *If potential being . . . sort of thing:* at line 4 Plotinus had raised the question whether an actual being is *eo ipso* an activity, but he had not raised a similar question concerning *dunamis*. At lines 21–23 the latter question is finally raised, once again via the classic example of the bronze and the statue: is it correct to say that the bronze is the power of the statue? The subsequent answer to this question is rather difficult to decipher, as the text oscillates between addressing two mistaken ways of conflating potential being and active power: the first consists, precisely, in saying that a potential being is *eo ipso* an active power, the second consists in saying that active powers are in potentiality (lines 26–28). The second claim, however, is not unrelated to the first: indeed, to say that active powers are in potentiality has as a consequence that not all, but at least some potential beings are active powers and correspond to activities.

1, 23–24 *If power is . . . not the case*: Plotinus' answer to the first hypothesis is straightforward, for if *dunamis* means the capacity to act, it would be absurd to think that the potential being bronze has this capacity. Bronze is said to be potential in relation to the statue only because it has the capacity to suffer a determinate kind of change, its potentiality is only passive. The agent is certainly not the bronze, but rather the sculptor, who can transform the bronze into a statue because he is the bearer of an active power, the capacity of sculpting, the realization of which is both the activity of sculpting and the final outcome of this activity, the bronze statue: see *Metaphysics* 9.8.1050a20–35. The example of bronze, therefore, makes it clear that a straightforward identification of potential being and active power is not possible.

1, 26–28 *However, if "potential . . . also in potentiality*: As already mentioned, the hypothesis that a potential being is by the same token an active power is reintroduced here from a different angle: active powers are in potentiality, which amounts to saying that at least some potential beings are at the same time active powers. For example, we might say that the capacity of learning in an uneducated man is in potentiality, and this would amount to saying that the capacity of learning is a potential being that is at the same time an active power. This possibility is quickly ruled out, without much of an explanation. Now, on what basis could somebody claim that active powers are in potentiality? A possible basis for such a view could be the conflation between a being that possesses a certain active faculty, and so can be considered in certain regards as a potential being, and the faculty itself: for example between a man who has the capacity of becoming a musician, and therefore is a musician in potentiality, and his capacity to learn music. This, however, is a mistake. It is certainly possible that Socrates has the capacity of undergoing a change of some sort: for example, he can become a musician, and therefore he is a musician in potentiality. However, Socrates should not be conflated with his capacity of learning, which is an active power of his soul, the realization of which is an activity. An active power, indeed, can never be considered as potential in the sense of passive potentiality. This is why Plotinus concludes that it is better and safer to establish a more rigorous correspondence between potential being and actual being, on the one hand, and power and act, on the other. Plotinus' provisional conclusion is then that *to dunamei* must be understood as related to *to energeiai*, and *dunamis* to *energeia* (lines 28–29).

At lines 27–28, the Greek text in HS_1 and HS_2 reads: *eiē an kai dunamis dunamei*, "then power is also in potentiality." Kirchhoff, followed by Theiler and Narbonne, added *to* before *dunamei* in order to attribute to *to dunamei* the role of the subject of the sentence (*eiē an kai dunamis* <*to*> *dunamei*). The rationale for this emendation is that the question asked by Plotinus at lines 21–23 is whether a potential being can be considered, by the same token, as an active power, and *not* whether active power is in potentiality. The emendation seems superfluous, however, because we can take lines 26–28 as an objection to the remark, made at lines 24–25, that an active power is not in potentiality. As we said, these lines offer a second perspective on the issue of the conflation between potential being and power. According to this perspective, if potential being were related not only to actual being, but also to activities, it would be legitimate to say, for example, that the faculty of sight is also sight in potentiality and thereby to consider the faculty of sight as a potential being that is also a power.

1, 29–34 Once he has established a precise distinction between the two different kinds of potentiality and the corresponding actualities, Plotinus mentions at the end of the chapter the Aristotelian definition of potential being as a substrate of the affections, forms, and shapes (*pathē, eidē, morphai*) that it is by nature ready to receive: Aristotle, *Metaphysics* 8.1.1042a32–b8 and 9.7.1049a29–39. Only once we have made a precise distinction between passive potentiality and active power is it possible to define—as Aristotle does—potential being as the substrate of a change consisting of receiving affections, forms, or shapes. Indeed, for Plotinus, the actualization of an active power is not a form of alteration.

I do not consider it necessary to identify here—as Narbonne does (1998, 44n25)—potential being as substrate with prime matter—and even less so if the context of this chapter is Aristotelian and the term *hupokeimenon* can therefore be understood in a broad sense as the mere substrate of a process of change (see the two meanings of *hupokeimenon* in *Metaphysics* 9.7.1049a29–39).

1, 31–32 *Moreover, potential beings strive to reach them*: This passage is rather obscure and has been translated in various ways; Vitringa and Theiler have even suggested some emendations. These emendations are not necessary and it is possible to make sense of this passage, while maintaining the text of the manuscripts. First of all, we can take *ta men,* in the sense of *ta men dunamei onta*, as the subject of *speudei elthein*, following the suggestion of HS_2. Second, we can take both *autōn* at line 33 and the relative pronoun *hōn* as referring to *ta de* [*dunamei onta*], and therefore to the potential beings. In this way, the meaning of the passage would be that potential beings, while already being something else in actuality, strive toward the forms, shapes, and affections that they are able to receive: but some strive toward perfection, while others strive toward corruption. *Speudei elthein* should not be understood in the sense of an activity of the potential being that goes toward the forms, for this would be at odds with the conclusions reached in the previous lines. It is rather to be understood as expressing a privation, and a passive predisposition, hence readiness, to receive forms and affections.

Chapter 2

The beginning of chapter 2 (lines 1–15) addresses two of the Aristotelian points mentioned in the first chapter at lines 10–21. The first point (lines 1–2)—the fact that a potential being is already another being in actuality—is here simply touched upon and will be developed in reference to prime matter only later, in chapters 4 and 5. The second point (lines 2–15)—that a potential being becomes an actual being either by remaining after the process of change or by being destroyed—is discussed immediately. The classic example of the bronze and the statue is again considered. Rather surprisingly, Plotinus concludes that, in a case of change such as the transformation of bronze into a statue, it is not possible to say in a proper sense that bronze is potentially the statue because it becomes *the statue. Indeed, the logos that is necessary for the production of the statue is not actually contained in the bronze: it is external, implying therefore a clear discontinuity between the preceding state—bronze—and the following state—the bronze statue.*

In the following lines (15–26) we find a second example, contrasted with the first: the case of the potential learned man who becomes an actual man of knowledge implies that the subject actualizing its capacity remains throughout and after the process of change. This observation allows Plotinus to give a more systematic answer to the very first questions raised in the first chapter (lines 1–6). In conclusion, we must distinguish, on the one hand, between 1) the substrate as potential being (to dunamei), *2) the compound of matter and form as actual being* (to energeiai) *and 3) the immanent form of a compound* (energeia toude). *And on the other hand, between 4) the possession of an active power* (dunamis) *and 5) the exercise of this active power* (energeia). *This systematization, however, is not exhaustive, as in chapter 3 Plotinus will articulate a further way of being in actuality, not corresponding to being in potentiality, namely the actual being of intelligible realities.*

2, 1–15 In these lines, Plotinus raises two different problems. The first is whether the Aristotelian observation that something potential is already something else in actuality holds in the case of prime matter as well. This question is only announced here, and will be addressed in detail only in chapters 4 and 5. Starting from line 3, Plotinus addresses the question of the passive potentiality of sensible objects. He suggests two alternative hypotheses. According to the first hypothesis, a potential thing *becomes* something actual, in other words it is actualized, when it receives a form and remains throughout the process of change. The reference here is not to qualitative change, but rather to the cases of change in which a new being comes to be, but the previous being is not entirely destroyed and remains as the substrate of the new compound, exemplified by the bronze and the statue. According to the second hypothesis, which represents Plotinus' own position, when a new, different being comes to be, we cannot say that a potential thing is actualized. When the statue is produced, bronze is not actualized because bronze does not contain in itself potentially the form of the statue, nor does it contain anything in its own nature that can announce the statue that will come to be, nor can it determine its own transfiguration. In order to speak of a passage from potential being to being in actuality, the way Aristotle does, one would need to suppose that the form of the statue is already contained in the bronze potentially. But this is not the case; on the contrary, the bronze needs to receive that form from something else, in this case from the sculptor. The sculptor, moreover, can give this *eidos* to the bronze because his soul has an active power, meaning an active capacity of shaping things according to preconceived forms. Properly speaking, then, bronze is not actualized in the process of change, for actuality belongs rather to the compound statue, in virtue of the form given to it by the sculptor. This is particularly evident in cases of change where the previous being is entirely destroyed during the process of change. What Plotinus implies here is that we cannot explain the phenomenal change in which a new being comes to be on the basis of horizontal causality. The fact that there is no passage from being in potentiality to being in actuality means further that there is no real continuity in the process of change. The potential being does not play any significant causal role. The only causality that plays a crucial role here is the active causality of the intelligible *logos*, namely a vertical causality, which breaks the continuity of change. This view is also clearly stated in a later treatise, *Enneads* VI.7 [38] 11, where Plotinus highlights that every generation, growth, and shaping is the effect of an active formative principle, and not of matter. For example, fire acts and generates itself through a rational principle able to give shapes and forms, and not through matter, since matter is not potentially a thing that can generate fire.

2, 1–2 *Concerning matter we . . . actuality at all*: Here Plotinus announces a question that he will investigate only in chapters 4 and 5. Although Plotinus does not use the expression *prōtē hulē* (prime matter), but only *hulē* (matter), he is referring specifically to prime matter, as it becomes clear in chapter 4. This is not unusual; Plotinus very often refers to prime matter when he uses the word *hulē* without further qualification: see for example *Ennead* II.4 [12]; III.6 [26]; and I.8 [51].

2, 3–4 *And in general . . . and remain themselves*: Plotinus begins addressing the question of the passive potentiality of sensible beings and suggests the first of the two hypotheses, according to which potential beings *become* something in actuality, when they receive a form and subsist through the process of change. I take *labonta to eidos kai menonta* ("when they receive a form and remain themselves") as indicating processes of generation in which the previous being becomes the matter of the new compound and therefore persists, such as the transfiguration of bronze or marble into a statue, of wood into a table, of wool into a sweater, and so on. Plotinus rejects this hypothesis for the reasons explained in the following lines.

2, 4–8 *whether "actual being". . . call "potential statue"*: According to the second hypothesis, which represents Plotinus' position, it is incorrect to say that a potential being *becomes* actual when a new thing comes to be. Plotinus reaches this conclusion, which is explicitly stated at lines 8–9, by once again examining the classical example of the bronze and the bronze statue. Bronze, which is already an actual being *qua* bronze, can be considered a "potential statue" on the basis of its capacity to become the matter of a new compound. However, it is not possible to attribute to bronze the actuality of the statue when it receives the shape of a statue, since the actuality of the statue must rather be predicated of the *compound*, newly constituted by the bronze and by the shape it received. The only actuality that can really be attributed to bronze is that which it already had, *qua* bronze. Moreover, as Christopher Noble (2013, 254) observes, the matter of a bronze statue is not qualified by the "statue-shape" at all, that is, the matter of a compound is not qualified by the form it underlies.

2, 8–10 *a potential being does not become actual*: this passage echoes Aristotle, *Physics* 1.7.190a20–30. Here Aristotle examines different ways that becoming is expressed in common language. In particular he distinguishes between two common expressions: "becoming that from this" (*ek tinos gignesthai ti*) and "this becoming that" (*tode gignesthai ti*). The first expression usually applies to the case of what does not survive the change, for example the case of a passage from contrary to contrary, let us say "from non-musical to musical." In this case, indeed, we can express the change in various ways: either by saying that "the non-musical becomes musical," or by saying that "the non-musical man becomes a musical man," or—precisely—by saying that "a musical man comes from a non-musical man." On the contrary, the latter expression does not usually apply to substrates, for they do not have contraries, and it does not usually apply to cases in which the substrate of change remains. For example, it is wrong to say that "from man becomes the musical," as man is the substance that remains, whereas it is the non-musical that disappears. However, there are some exceptions. For instance, it is commonly said that "the statue comes from bronze," and not that "bronze becomes a statue," in spite of the fact that bronze is a substrate and that it remains through the change. Plotinus draws a radical conclusion from this observation. If, in the case of bronze, it is more correct to say that a statue comes to be from the bronze, rather than to say that the bronze becomes a statue, this is because it is not the case that this potential being becomes an actual being. In other words the transfiguration of bronze is not the realization of the passive potentiality of bronze, but rather that of the active power of the sculptor.

2, 10–11 *the actual being... on the other*: For the translation of this passage I follow the indication of HS_2. While it might appear surprising that in this line Plotinus is denying that the form is an actual being (*to energeiai*), we will discover at the end of the chapter that the proper way to refer to the form is to consider it as an act (*energeia*). Here, therefore, Plotinus is suggesting that only the compound should be considered an actual being, not its matter or the form imposed upon it.

2, 12–13 *And this is . . . the bronze statue*: This is an important specification. The reasoning just developed holds whenever a substance is produced anew, that is, whenever we have a process of change that in Aristotelian terms should be defined as "substantial change," but in Plotinian terms is defined as "the coming to be of a new thing." Plotinus specifies that the statue as a compound is another, new, different *ousia* with regard to bronze. The potential thing is something different from the new actual thing produced by the process of change. This specification might indicate that the reasoning according to which a potential being is not actualized in the process of change holds only in the case of generation of a new *this*, but not in the case of alterations. It is rather difficult to say if this is the case, since, as we will soon discover, Plotinus does not address the question of qualitative change in this treatise.

Narbonne gives an opposite reading of this passage: according to him Plotinus challenges the distinction between substantial and qualitative change, particularly at lines 12–15, since in this passage *every* becoming-other is reduced to an *absolute* becoming-other (1998, 79). According to this reading, then, Plotinus denies all continuity between potentiality and actuality in every kind of change, for in each case actuality would be the actual existence of a new substance. The example provided at line 15, the production of another new substance, would be the model on the basis of which we must understand every process of change in the physical world, the consequence of this view being that Plotinus is proposing in this passage a totally "discontinuist" model against the Peripatetic "continuist" model of becoming (see Narbonne 1998, 87). This reading is grounded in Plotinus' argument for the non-substantial nature of sensible objects and their pseudo-hylomorphism: because Plotinus rejects Aristotelian hylomorphism—an issue that we will examine in detail later—sensible objects are for him nothing but conglomerates of qualities and matter, and therefore every change in their configuration must be understood as an absolute change. That is, bronze is not a unified compound of matter and form and is not able to remain through the change of its accidents, but rather is only a group of spatialized qualities that in every process of change is replaced by another particular group of qualities standing for the new compound. Narbonne borrows from Gerson the simile of the film reel to explain the discontinous nature of this change (see Gerson 1994, 112). A film reel is made up of a succession of separate frames. Only during the projection does the flow of the film reel give to the eye watching it the impression of continuity, which is actually only phenomenal, related simply to the way in which the flow of the film reel is grasped by sense-perception, but not based on the real nature of the film reel itself. In other words, the projection on a screen gives the impression of a continuity of movement, but this does not allow the spectator to assert that the previous frame is potentially the following one.

While the image of the film reel may satisfactorily describe the way generation works for Plotinus, we do not have any textual evidence in this treatise to claim that this is the way all processes of change should be understood. Indeed, until now Plotinus has never addressed alterations: all his examples are examples of substantial change in Aristotelian terms (see above, the discussion of 1, 17–21). We have seen that for Aristotle a change of shape of the kind the bronze undergoes should be understood as a substantial change, and in these lines Plotinus is clearly indicating that he understands this change as the coming to be of a new substance.

To summarize, in these lines Plotinus does not criticize the Peripatetic distinction between qualitative and substantial change. Moreover, from the fact that Plotinus denies any substantiality to sensible beings, as they have a phantom nature and remain dependent on the intelligible realm (on this subject see below, the commentary on chapter 5), it does not follow that Plotinus does not distinguish different kinds of change. On the contrary, we can still suppose a differentiation between changes that require the replacement of the previous *logos* with a new *logos* and changes that do not require this.

In conclusion, the reasoning developed in these lines is certainly a critique of Aristotle, but this critique concerns only the cases of change that, in Aristotelian terms, should be defined as substantial. It consists of denying any continuity between the potential being and the new actual being that comes to be from it, and in stating a model of vertical causality instead of horizontal causality whenever a new thing comes to be. See Kalligas (2014, *ad loc.*) for an interpretation similar to mine.

2, 14 *And in the case . . . not remain at all*: This line addresses the case of generation of a new *this* in which the previous thing does not remain through the process of change, like the examples of water becoming bronze, and air becoming fire mentioned in chapter 1, 21: in these cases, the discontinuity in the process of change is all the more evident.

2, 15–26 The conclusion of the first part of chapter 2 is that there is discontinuity between a potential being and an actual being when a new *ousia* comes to be in the physical realm. Once this conclusion is reached, Plotinus raises the question of whether this also applies to alterations concerning the soul; for in this case it would seem that the subject that undergoes the alteration remains nonetheless the same. Indeed, in this kind of change, the substrate of change is the soul, which acquires a new state (being learned) in virtue of its inner predisposition to acquire knowledge. This entails continuity throughout the process of change, because 1) the soul remains the same, and 2) by learning, the soul realizes its own predisposition to knowledge.

The basis for this reflection is Aristotle, *On the Soul* 2.5.417a–b. Here Aristotle distinguishes three states of the soul. When we say: "being a man of knowledge," this can have three different meanings: i) A man is a "man of knowledge" because he belongs to the human kind, which has the capacity of acquiring knowledge by virtue of its intelligence. ii) A man is a "man of knowledge" because he has acquired knowledge, for example through education: he, therefore, is a learned man in the sense of having been educated and possessing knowledge. iii) A man is a "man of knowledge" because he is actually using the knowledge he has acquired: in this case he is a man of knowledge in actuality. The states i) and ii) correspond to two different ways of being in potentiality. Indeed while it is true that state ii) is the actualization of state i), and in this sense is an *energeia*, it is also true that it is in potentiality with respect to state iii). According to the Aristotelian doctrine of the ontological priority of actuality over potentiality the actuality, then, state iii)—the active exercise of knowledge—is superior to state ii). We will see in chapter 3 that for Plotinus this is not the case.

According to Aristotle, in order to change from state i) to state ii), a man must undergo an alteration, for he needs to realize, through education and learning, a potentiality that belongs to him as a member of the human kind. He, therefore, must undergo a change from contrary to contrary: from being unlearned to being learned. The man in state ii) already possesses knowledge: the realization of this possession, that is, the exercise of his knowledge, does not entail any alteration or any passage from contrary to contrary. Indeed, by exercising his knowledge in actuality the man of knowledge does not acquire more knowledge than he already has. From state ii) to state iii), therefore, no alteration takes place. The consequence of this is that the activity of thinking, or the activity of the architect when he builds, does not entail an alteration in the thinking man or in the architect. Moreover, the realization of their faculties does not entail a destruction of those faculties: on the contrary, a man who thinks in actuality thereby preserves his capacity for thinking. In other words, the being in potentiality is preserved in the being in actuality.

These Aristotelian distinctions can be recognized in our Plotinian passage. From line 15 to line 22, we find the explanation of the passage from state i) to state ii), as a realization of the soul's predisposition to knowledge. At lines 22–26, Plotinus addresses the passage from state ii) to state iii), and in particular the fact that the potentially learned man is preserved in the actually learned man. In a learned man in actuality, indeed, the potentiality of exercising his knowledge is joined to its form, namely, the act of exercising it.

2, 19–20 *Rather, the unlearned . . . knowledge by accident*: *ē* ("rather") at the beginning of the sentence has a disjunctive function with adversative meaning. It indicates that these lines are to be taken as a negative answer to the hypothesis that the unlearned man is potentially a man of knowledge. Indeed, properly speaking this is not the case. The potentiality of acquiring knowledge belongs to man, or, to be more precise, to the soul, and not to the unlearned. This is why it is only by accident that the unlearned becomes a man of knowledge. First of all, being unlearned is an accidental state for man, who has the capacity of being both, learned and unlearned. Second, becoming learned is the realization of a faculty or of a predisposition of the soul, and not of a potentiality inherent in the fact of being unlearned. In this process, the substrate of change is man, who passes from contrary to contrary, from being unlearned to being a man of knowledge, and who remains through the change.

2, 21–22 *while the potential being was the soul*: It is unnecessary to emend the text and to delete *to* before *dunamei*, following Creuzer, Theiler and Narbonne. Their emendation might be justified by the fact that in chapter 3 Plotinus will deny that *to dunamei*, in the sense of passive potentiality, can be referred to the soul. However, at this stage of chapter 2, Plotinus has not articulated his arguments regarding the impossibility of attributing passive potentiality to intelligible realities yet. Here Plotinus objects that the potential being is not the unlearned, but rather the soul, that is, that the potentiality lies not in the fact of being unlearned, but rather in the soul. This is the core of the argument of these lines, while the issue of whether it is correct to define the soul as a *to dunamei*, or whether it is more correct to define it as a *dunamis*, will be addressed and solved only later. Following

Igal, I take *to dunamei* to be the subject and *hēiper* ("in virtue of which") to refer to *psuchē . . . epitēdeiōs echousa* ("the soul, as it had in itself a convenient predisposition"). It is in virtue of the predisposition of his soul to acquire knowledge that the unlearned man becomes a man of knowledge in actuality. We will then discover in chapter 3 that this predisposition must be understood as an active power, and not as a *to dunamei*.

2, 22 *actually*: Here *kai* has the meaning of "actually" (see Denniston 1954, 316-321).

2, 24 *in actuality*: As in 1, 17, *ēdē* indicates being in actuality.

2, 26–36 In the first section of chapter 2 Plotinus addressed the case of change in the physical realm in which a new thing comes to be, and in the second section he dealt with the question of potentiality and alteration with respect to the soul. In the last section, he finally reaches a definitive conclusion concerning the distinction between passive potentiality and active power and their relation to different forms of actuality. By doing so he offers an answer to the first two questions asked at the beginning of chapter 1: i) what are potential and actual being? And ii) are actual being and activity identical? Moreover, he recapitulates a series of conclusions already reached in both chapters. In 1, 28–29, Plotinus had already stressed that, while *to dunamei* properly relates to *to energeiai*, *dunamis* properly relates to *energeia*. After having clarified the proper correlations among those four terms, it remained to discover what precisely those terms indicate. In 2, 10–11, we discovered that *to energeiai* is the compound of matter and form, and that neither the matter nor the immanent form alone (i.e., the form upon matter) can be considered as actual being. In the conclusion of the chapter, we finally discover that *to dunamei* is the substrate of change, while *to energeiai* is the compound of matter and form that is related to it. These observations must be taken as referring to sensible objects alone, for, as we will see, the Forms in the intelligible realm are both actual beings and activities.

We then learn that *dunamis* is a *hexis*, an active disposition, as for example the virtue of courage. *Energeia*, instead, can have two meanings. First, it indicates the form (*eidos*) and in this case we should rather speak of the *energeia toude*, of the actuality or activity of a determinate thing. In other words, according to this first meaning, *energeia* is the form in virtue of which a compound is the determinate kind of thing that it is. This use, however, is somewhat improper, for the proper use of the term *energeia* is the second, which refers to the exercise of an active power. One can better understand Plotinus' view if one takes into account his distinction between immanent form as a static form and the "awakened form" (*eidos egrēgoros*) as movement (see Chiaradonna 2002, 203–204). For the Plotinian solution to the problem of the relationship between actuality and "to act," see Taormina (1999, 103–106).

The main difference in the way that potential being relates to actual being and active power relates to activity is that a potential being needs a form coming from something else, which for Plotinus entails some radical consequences concerning the continuity of change, as we have seen. On the contrary, an active power realizes itself by itself: as Aristotle clarifies in *On the Soul* 2.5.417a25–30, for its realization it is sufficient that no external impediments are in place. This is the reason why, according to Aristotle, the actualization of this kind of power, which Plotinus equates to a *hexis*, does not imply any alteration. This point, as we will see, is a key aspect of Plotinus' treatment of *dunamis* in the intelligible realm, in the following chapter.

Chapter 3

This chapter is the heart of the treatise. As Plotinus specifies at the very beginning (line 1), the conceptual differentiation between different forms of dunamis *and* energeia *developed in the previous chapters was intended as a premise to the treatment of the core issue of the treatise, namely: how do* dunamis *and* energeia *apply to the case of the intelligible realities? The rest of chapter 3 is devoted to answering this question, starting from the problem of potential being. Plotinus immediately excludes the possibility that potential being applies to the intelligible realm, and in order to prove this point he addresses and solves two controversial cases that might seem to introduce being in potentiality among the intelligible realities: the case of intelligible matter and that of the soul that undergoes change.*

The subsequent part of the chapter focuses on the identification between being in actuality and being an activity both in the case of each of the intelligible realities taken singularly and in the case of them taken as a whole. The chapter ends with a praise of the intelligible realm that echoes Plato's Timaeus *and* Phaedrus.

3, 1–4 Plotinus begins this chapter by exhorting himself and his readers to go back to the "question for the sake of which these things (*tauta*) have been said by way of preface." If we take *en tois ousi* (among the beings) in 1, 2 as referring not to beings or realities in general, but rather to intelligible realities more specifically, then we might say that Plotinus is exhorting us to go back to the opening question of the treatise, namely: how should we speak of actuality and potentiality in the case of intelligible reality? In order to be able to answer this question, it was first necessary to revise the Aristotelian conceptual framework concerning *dunamis* and *energeia* and to introduce clearer distinctions among their different forms, and in particular between the active and the passive sense of these terms. This is the task performed by chapters 1 and 2. We can, therefore, see here how the treatment of phenomena of change in the sensible realm in chapters 1 and 2, albeit very sophisticated, cannot be taken as an aim in itself. Indeed, by referring to the way potentiality and actuality are at work in the sensible realm, we can then ascend to the intelligible, by way both of contrast and of analogy. However, the fact that the consideration of the sensible world is a means to rather than an aim of Plotinus' investigation does not entail that his natural philosophy is of no theoretical interest. On the contrary, as Wildberg put it: "although it would certainly be false to say that Plotinus was a natural scientist in the same sense in which Aristotle, Galen, or Ptolemy can be called 'scientists,' it seems nevertheless right to affirm both that Plotinus was a keen and shrewd observer of the phenomena, and that he tackled fundamental questions of natural philosophy in earnest, if in his own idiosyncratic way" (Wildberg 2009, 122).

In lines 2–4, Plotinus asks a series of four questions: i) In what way do we speak of being in actuality among the intelligible realities (lines 1–2)? ii) Is each of the intelligible realities only in actuality, or is each of them an activity as well (lines 2–3)? iii) Is the totality of intelligible realities an activity (line 3)? iv) And, finally, is there being in potentiality among intelligible realities (lines 4–5)?

3, 3 *Taken together as . . . are they activity?* Plotinus distinguishes between intelligible realities taken singularly and taken as a whole. This distinction is not superfluous, insofar as for Plotinus the whole is not equivalent to the mere addition of the parts and the whole and the parts correspond to two different ontological levels: there is, indeed, an ontological hierarchy between the whole and the parts, where the whole is superior to the parts. This view can be better explained by examining Plotinus' classic example of a science and of its theorems. We can find this example in several passages of the *Enneads*, where it is used to clarify the relation between unity and multiplicity in the case both of Intellect and the individual intellects, and of the Whole Soul and the individual souls: *Ennead* V.9.8, 3–7; IV.9.5; III.9.2; VI.4.16, 24–32; IV.3.2, 50–54; VI.2.20, 1–29. The analogy works in this way: the whole Intellect and the whole Soul give themselves to the individual intellects and to the individual souls by remaining one, without losing anything of themselves, and without being diminished, in the same way a science (*epistēmē*) is divided into single theorems, while remaining one and entire, and each theorem contains the whole science in potentiality. Christian Tornau has given a convincing interpretation of this rather puzzling analogy (1998). Indeed, what does it mean that a single theorem contains the whole science in potentiality? According to Tornau, this analogy is better understood if referred to a scientist having knowledge of a science and using it; moreover, we need to combine the notions of potentiality and actuality with the Stoic distinction between *logos endiathetos* (the word remaining within, i.e. in the soul) and *logos prophorikos* (the uttered word). In Plotinus' view, the *logos prophorikos* is an actualization of the *logos endiathetos*. A single theorem uttered, explained, or taught by a scientist is like a *logos prophorikos*, an utterance of a *logos* contained within his soul, and is a partial actualization of the whole science to which it belongs, that is, it is a partial actualization of the knowledge of the scientist. Think, for example, of a scientist explaining a geometry theorem to a student: while he has the whole science within his soul (as this is necessary for him to be a scientist), he utters and explains only a single part of this science, for example Pythagoras' theorem. By teaching this single theorem he is, therefore, actualizing only one part of his capacity: indeed, as we said, he knows the whole geometry, although he is not using all his knowledge at the moment. On the other hand, the scientific character of a single theorem depends on the whole. This means two things: the first is that it is by belonging to a whole that a single theorem has a scientific value; the second is that it is the knowledge of the whole, and not the utterance of a single theorem, that determines the fact that the person who is uttering the theorem is a scientist. A parrot repeating a theorem is not a scientist and the theorem uttered by it has no scientific value. What is the conclusion of all this? A theorem is a partial actualization of a science, understood as an active power or capacity within the soul of the scientist: since it is only a partial, and not a complete, actualization of an active power that goes beyond it, the theorem is inferior to the whole science and to this active *dunamis*, with a typical Plotinian inversion of the Aristotelian priority of actuality over potentiality. We will see later how this inversion applies to the case of the soul. The science analogy was meant to explain the way Intellect relates to the individual intellects and the whole Soul relates to the individual souls. To sum up, there is a hierarchy between these two levels, Intellect and whole Soul, on the one hand, and individual intellects and individual souls, on the other, insofar as the latter are—like single uttered theorems—actualizations of the *dunamis* of the Intellect and of the whole Soul.

3, 4–22 In 1, 6–10, Plotinus had already asked the question whether there is potential being among intelligible realities and he had already offered a rather provisional answer: there cannot be potential being there because of the absence of time. The answer provided in chapter 3 concludes with the same argument—the absence of time—but adds two further specifications. We cannot speak of potential being if in the intelligible realm there is no matter where this potential being might reside (line 4) and if there is no possibility of change (lines 4–8). This latter point is particularly important, as on the basis of Aristotle's notion of being in potentiality, the passage from being in potentiality to being in actuality entails change. Supposing that intelligible realities are in potentiality would then equate to making them deficient and corruptible, and to introduce becoming into the intelligible realm. In *Ennead* III.7.7, 12–16, for example, Plotinus writes: "If this is so, there is nothing that is going to be for it; for, if something is going to be, it was lacking to it before; so it was not the whole" (translation: Armstrong). As intelligible realities are perfect, they do not lack anything and they are eternal and not in time, they are not about to become something else and therefore they are not potential.

Once the solution to the question has been provided, Plotinus needs to address two possible objections. The first concerns the case of intelligible matter: indeed, if, as Plotinus does in *Ennead* II.4 [12], we admit that there is such a thing as intelligible matter, how can we deny that this matter is in potentiality? It would seem that being in potentiality is precisely what characterizes matter and distinguishes it from form. As we will see, Plotinus' answer to this question consists of stating the difference between intelligible and sensible matter, and in asserting that intelligible matter is not only always united to its form, but it is of the same nature as the form, from which it is distinguished only conceptually (lines 13–18).

The second objection concerns the soul: it would seem that the soul does undergo change, for example it can become a living being, through embodiment, and it can become musical, through education (lines 19–21). But in order to be able to change into a living being or into a musical soul, the soul must be a living being and a musical soul in potentiality. Moreover, in the case of the soul, the argument concerning the absence of time can hardly be applied: as Plotinus explains in III.7.11, the soul is not only the source of time, but it also temporalizes itself, because of its restlessness and self-assertion, which lead it to separate itself from Intellect. Indeed, the lower soul produces the sensible world in time and orders it through time. Plotinus' point is not that the nature of the soul is temporal, as the soul is and remains eternal, but rather that its operations and the life it leads, *when it leaves the intelligible realm*, are in time. In the case of the individual soul, moreover, we have not only time, but it would seem that we have also change, as the individual soul, albeit eternal, does not always perform the same activity (see IV.4.17). Plotinus' answer to this objection consists of contrasting potential being with active power. It is wrong to say that the soul is potentially musical, as it is more correct to say that the soul has the power to be musical: becoming musical is, then, the actualization of an active *dunamis* (line 22) and does not entail a deficiency of the soul.

3, 5 *something that it is not already*: "Already," *ēdē* indicates the eternity of the intelligible realities.

3, 5–6 *if nothing gives . . . what it is*: The two alternatives here correspond to the distinction between two different kinds of substantial change in 1, 18–21.

I follow HS_5 and the manuscript family y: *mēde ti*, and not *mēd'eti* (HS_2).

3, 12–13 *what will we answer?*: I follow the manuscript family y and Narbonne (1998, 51n53): *eroumen* ("will we answer"), and not *erousin* ("will they answer"), which is reported in all the other manuscript families and in HS_2. Indeed, as Narbonne rightly emphasizes, Plotinus is among the proponents of the theory of intelligible matter, as it appears clearly both in II.4 [12] and in the subsequent lines of this chapter, where he appears to be concerned by the objection about the presence of potential being in intelligible matter and he offers an answer to this objection. See also *eroumen* later, at line 19: "But concerning the soul, what shall we answer?"

The notion of intelligible matter had been elaborated particularly within the Middle Platonic philosophical tradition (see, for example, Numenius, fr. 11). The doctrine was based on Aristotle's identification between material cause and the Dyad: in *Metaphysics* 1.6.987b–988a, indeed, Aristotle reports that, according to Plato, Forms and Numbers derive from two primary principles, the One and the indeterminate Dyad, where the first is a formal cause and the second a material cause—a substrate. The Dyad would then be intelligible matter. In the *Enneads* we can find references to both the Dyad (for example, in V.4.2, 7–8; V.1.5, 6–8; VI.7.8, 22ff.) and intelligible matter. Plotinus' theory of intelligible matter is developed in particular in II.4 [12]. Here, at the beginning of the treatise, Plotinus refers to the fact that some philosophers argue that if there is sensible matter, then there must be a corresponding matter in the intelligible realm, where matter is the substrate of the Forms and of incorporeal substances: II.4 [12] 1, 14–18. Plotinus, then, lists a series of possible objections to the existence of intelligible matter: "If what is of the matter kind must be something undefined and shapeless, and there is nothing undefined or shapeless among the beings there, which are the best, there would not be matter there. And if every intelligible being is simple, there would be no need of matter, so that the composite being might come from it and from something else. And there is need of matter for beings that come into existence and are made into one thing after another—this was what led people to conceive the matter of beings perceived by the senses—but not for beings that do not come into existence. And where did it come from? From where did it get its being? If it came to be, it was by some agency; but if it was eternal, there would be several principles and the primary beings would exist by chance. And if form comes to matter, the composite being will be a body; so that there will be body in the intelligible world too" (II.4.2, translation: Armstrong). The following three chapters, 3–5, are devoted to answering these questions and arguing in favor of the existence of intelligible matter, while the rest of the treatise (chapters 6–16) focuses on sensible matter: the last two references to intelligible matter are in II.4.5, 24–28 and in II.4.15, 17–37, within the discussion of the nature of the infinite. Plotinus' main argument in favor of the existence of intelligible matter relies on the necessity of a common substrate for the multiplicity of Forms within Intellect. The multiplicity of Forms is the determination of a common, indeterminate substrate: "If, then, the Forms are many, there must be something in them common to them all; and also something individual, by which one differs from another. Now, this something individual, this separating difference, is the shape which belongs to each. But if there is a shape, there is that which is shaped, about which the difference is predicated. Therefore, there is matter which receives the shape, and is the substrate in every case" (II.4.4, 2–7, translation: Armstrong). On the basis of this passage, it appears that intelligible reality, albeit not corporeal, is nonetheless a compound. This notion also recurs in II.5.3, 11–12. In II.4 [12], Plotinus is particularly concerned with the possible objection that, if considered as a compound, intelligible reality can then be conceived of as a body, composed of separable parts: an objection to which he responds by insisting on the peculiar relation between unity and multiplicity that characterizes Intellect in contrast to sensible beings. A second powerful objection is that, if speaking of intelligible matter is to have some meaning, then we need to attribute indeterminacy, lack of form, and obscurity to intelligible matter. Plotinus' solution to this problem consists of insisting, first, that since there is no becoming, intelligible matter is always already united to its Form; and second, that in contrast to sensible matter, intelligible matter is a substance (*ousia*: II 4.4, 22).

For a detailed discussion of intelligible matter and its role in Plotinus' work, see Narbonne (1993, 47–134) and Perdikouri (2014, 89–130).

3, 13 *What is there . . . is a form*: the claim that intelligible matter is a form echoes II.4.3, 22, where Plotinus says that intelligible matter, in contrast to sensible matter, is a substance (*ousia*).

ē introduces the answer and is not disjunctive (*contra* Narbonne 1998, 51n54).

3, 13–14 *since even the . . . to something else*: the soul is matter in the sense that it is the receptacle of the noetic contents coming from Intellect: in this sense the soul is matter, whereas the Intellect toward which the soul turns itself is its form. See, for example, V.1.3, 20–25 and V.9.3, 20–22: "And then again you will enquire whether the soul is one of the simple entities, or whether there is something in it like matter and something like form, the intellect in it [. . .]" (translation: Armstrong).

3, 14–15 *Then, will it . . . that something else?*: It is unclear what the subject is. From a grammatical viewpoint the subject might be *psuchē* at line 14. However, the soul is introduced at line 14 only as an example, and the real discussion about the soul begins only later, at line 19. This is why the more plausible subject for this sentence is intelligible matter, as suggested by Narbonne (1998, 51n56).

3, 15 *For we did . . . is its form*: *Eidos gar ēn autēs*: From a grammatical viewpoint, this sentence might be understood as an unreal condition without *an* (which is grammatically possible, especially in Plotinus). This is the way Armstrong translates it: "for then the something else would be its form." However, as noted by Narbonne, from a conceptual viewpoint this translation does not make sense, as in the subsequent lines Plotinus not only does not deny that "that something else" is the form of intelligible matter, but insists on considering the intelligible reality as conceptually distinguished into matter and form. See Narbonne (1998, 52n57). The use of the imperfect tense, *ēn*, might be understood as referring to the fact that Plotinus has already mentioned, a few lines earlier, the form of intelligible matter: *ēn* can then be rendered as "For we did say that . . . is."

3, 15 *and yet*: For the combination *kai . . . de*, see Denniston (1954, 199).

3, 15–16 *this form does . . . separated except conceptually*: Because of the absence of time and change in the intelligible world, intelligible matter is always united to its form. The same concept is articulated in II.4.3, 9–11: "The matter, too, of the things that came into being is always receiving different forms, but the matter of eternal things is always the same and always has the same form" (translation: Armstrong); and a few lines later, 13–14: "But in the intelligible world matter is all things at once; so it has nothing to change into, for it has all things already" (translation: Armstrong). Since intelligible matter is always united with its form, it is not about to become anything different from what it already is and it has no lack or deficiency, so it is certainly not potential in this sense.

3, 16–17 *and it is . . . matter as well*: The subject of *echon* is unclear. According to Narbonne the subject is the form (1998, 52n58). This option, however, is unconvincing, as immediately after Plotinus refers to what is conceived of as divided into two parts, and this cannot be the form. The subject of *echon* is, then, most likely *to sunamphoteron* at line 12, the compound, that is, intelligible reality.

3, 18–19 *Aristotle says that quintessence is immaterial*: This sentence is so puzzling that Igal considered it a scolium interpolated into the text (1982, *ad loc.*). Indeed, in *On the Heavens* (*De Caelo*) Aristotle does not say that the celestial substance is immaterial, but rather that it is impassible, incorruptible, unchanging: see *On the Heavens* 1.3.270a–b. Armstrong suggests that "possibly Plotinus depends here on some Peripatetic commentator on this passage, who drew the conclusion that Aristotle thought that the quintessence was without matter because he states so clearly that it is absolutely unchanging, and there is therefore no need to postulate any matter in it to be the substrate of change" (*ad loc.*).

3, 19 *For it is a living being in potentiality*: In a much later treatise, I.1 [53], Plotinus defines the living being (*zōion*) as the living body, the compound of the body and of an image coming from the soul, which organizes the body as a living and coherent organism: I.1.7, 1–6. Partially following Aristotle's *On the Soul* 1.4.408b10–13, Plotinus asserts that the subject of affections, sensation, bodily desires, and sufferings is not the soul, but rather the *zōion*. But, contrary to Aristotle, he holds that the soul is an extrinsic cause vivifying the body through an image of itself.

In 3, 19–20, Plotinus voices a possible interpretation of the relationship between body and soul that would imply that the soul is a potential being as it can become a *zōion*. Indeed, one might understand the descent of the soul into a body as a transformation of the soul and therefore as a passage from potential being to actual being. However, as clearly stated at line 22, this is not the case, and it is rather more correct to say that the soul is the power of the living being. In order to understand what this means, we can refer to Plotinus' explanation of the way the soul is present to the body in IV.3.22 and 23. Here Plotinus uses the notion of *dunamis* to clarify that the soul is present to the whole body, to all its parts, without being *in* the body: "We must not say that there is even a presence of the other powers of soul to the body, but that the powers which it needs are present, and present without being situated in its parts, or in the whole either, and the sense-faculty is present to the whole of the perceiving body for the purposes of sense-perception, but one part at one time to one and one to another according to the [particular] sense-activity [which is going on]" (*Enn.* IV.3.22, 12–17, translation: Armstrong). It is through the powers transmitted by the soul that the living body can sense: while the soul in itself is not localized in any part of the body, it gives specific *dunameis* to specific parts of the body, which will accomplish specific tasks. The power of sight will be in the eyes, that of smell in the nostrils, and the power to set the living body in motion will be in the nerves and in the brain. By resorting to the idea that the soul gives its powers to the different parts of the body in a differential way, Plotinus can avoid a tripartite notion of the soul and assert instead its fundamental unity. The notion of the *dunamis* of the soul as the principle of the body's capacity to sense and to move is restated in I.1.6, where Plotinus points out that the powers of the soul, while responsible for the movement of the living being, remain in themselves unmoved. This view allows Plotinus to reject the Aristotelian notion of the soul as the form of a body and to assert the ontological independence of the soul from the body.

3, 20 *is musical in potentiality*: As we have already seen, in *On the Soul* 2.5.417a–b Aristotle distinguishes between two kinds of potentiality of a man in relation to knowledge: a man is potentially learned because he has the capacity of learning due to his belonging to his *genos*, and this is the first kind of potentiality. The second kind is when a man, who has already acquired knowledge, is not actually using his knowledge: this kind of potentiality, the possession of knowledge, is at the same time an actuality (*entelecheia*) or, more specifically, "first actuality" (*On the Soul* 2.1.412a22–28).

In Plotinus' eyes the consideration of the first kind of potentiality might lead to misunderstandings, such as thinking that since the soul has the capacity to become musical, it is subject to alteration, and therefore is in potentiality in the sense of passive potentiality. Aristotle himself had pointed out the difficulty of describing the potentiality for knowledge as the capacity of "being acted upon": "and that which, starting with a potentiality for knowledge, learns and acquires knowledge from what is actual and able to teach, either ought not to be described as 'being acted upon,' as has been said, or else there are two senses of alteration, one a change to a negative condition, and the other a change to a positive state, that is, a realization of its nature" (*On the Soul* 2.5.417b12–16, translation: Hett). While the passage from not having knowledge to having knowledge implies an alteration and a change from contrary to contrary, it is a specific kind of alteration, consisting in the realization of one's nature.

3, 20–21 *and all those . . . at all times*: The individual soul, contrary to the Soul and to the soul of the world, in spite of being eternal, since it descends into the body, is not always engaged in the same kind of activities. Indeed, the individual soul has an amphibious nature, since it is intelligible but must be able to act in the sensible world as well: "Because this nature is twofold, both intelligible and sensible, it is better for the soul to have its being in the intelligible world; but even so, since it has the sort of nature it has, it must of necessity have the ability to participate in the sensible world as well, and it should not feel aggrieved with itself, in that it is not superior in all respects, for holding a middle rank among real being" (IV.8.7, 1–6, translation: Fleet). Elsewhere in this treatise, Plotinus clarifies that one of the reasons why the descent of the individual soul is necessary is that by doing so the soul displays and realizes powers that would have remained latent in the intelligible world (IV.8.5, 24–33). Since, by ensouling a body, the soul is actualizing some powers that it would not actualize if it were to remain in the intelligible realm, one might say that in a sense the soul is in potentiality. Not in the sense of being able to be acted upon, but rather in the sense of realizing something that did not exist before in actuality. In the case of the capacity of learning music, for example, it is clear that the soul comes to be something that, because of its descent into a body, it was not before. Only in this specific sense can one attribute potential being to the soul, without thereby implying any passive potentiality. On this point see Dufour (2004, 214).

3, 22 *the soul is . . . of these things*: As we have already mentioned, Plotinus' solution to the problem of the potentiality of the individual soul is to insist on the active nature of this potentiality. The description of the soul as *dunamis toutōn* (the power of these things) can be better understood if we refer to the *dunamis* of the One, defined by Plotinus as *dunamis pantōn* (power of everything) in several occasions throughout the *Enneads* (see, for example, V.4.2; V.1.7, 9–10; V.3.15, 33). Plotinus introduces the notion of *dunamis pantōn* in order to explain how the One can be the source and efficient cause of everything, without being altered by the process of derivation of the whole reality from it and without being considered as in potentiality, and therefore as imperfect or deficient. The active power of the One, indeed, is grounded in its perfection and not in its deficiency. In V.4 [7], the perfection of the One is indicated as the reason why everything is generated from it, since perfection and fecundity are strictly bound together: it is precisely because it is perfect and superabundant that the One has effects outside of itself. On this topic see Aubry (2000) and Aubry (2006, 215–247). In V.5.12, 44–47 this idea is further explained through a reference to the absence of jealousy (*aphtonia*) in god in Plato's *Timaeus* 29e.

The power of the One is transmitted to the other intelligible levels and to the sensible world, like a universal life that vivifies everything. Indeed, the power of the One is not only a generative power that keeps everything alive and organized together as in a living organism, but it is also the paradigm of every generation and of all efficient causality: "How then does it come from the First? If the First is perfect, the most perfect of all, and the primal power, it must be the most powerful of all beings and the other powers must imitate it as far as they are able. Now when anything else comes to perfection we see that it produces, and does not endure to remain by itself, but makes something else. This is true not only of things which have choice, but of things which grow and produce without choosing to do so, and even lifeless things, which impart themselves to others as far as they can: as fire warms, snow cools, and drugs act on something else in a way corresponding to their nature—all imitating the First Principles as far as they are able by tending to everlastingness and generosity" (V.4.1, 23–34, translation: Armstrong).

Like every other being, the soul receives its power from the One. This is a power based on the very being and nature of the soul, and decoupled from notions of deficiency or imperfection.

3, 22–40 The second part of the chapter deals with the *energeia* of the intelligible realm, by addressing two questions: first, in what sense can we speak of actual being among intelligible realities; second, whether intelligible beings are both in actuality and activities, and how. *Energeia* plays an important role in Plotinus' conception of the intelligible realm. All intelligible realities, while being active powers, are always in actuality: their being in actuality is, indeed, the expression of their perfection and self-sufficiency. Their actuality, however, should not be understood as the outcome of a process of change from potential being to actual being, as in the case of a sensible compound, such as a bronze statue, but rather as an activity of self-constitution, or inner activity.

While there is no explicit mention of the doctrine of the double *energeia* in II.5, it is useful to refer to it in order to clarify why the notion of *energeia*, understood in its double meaning of actual being and activity, plays a crucial role in Plotinus' understanding of the intelligible realm. Plotinus refers to double activity in several passages of the *Enneads*, for example: V.4.2; V.1.3, 10–12; 6, 30–39; V.3.7. The notion of double activity enables him to give an account of a kind of causality grounded in the very nature of intelligible beings and not implying any change or affection in the cause. We can distinguish, on the one hand, an inner activity or first activity, which is the act through which a reality constitutes itself: the inner activity of each thing defines this thing, is a self-contained act and is not changed by acting. This inner activity can also be identified with the active power of intelligible realities. On the other hand, the second activity is an other-directed act, an external outcome flowing necessarily from the first activity. In order to explain this concept,

Plotinus often refers to the fire analogy: the first activity can be identified with the being of fire itself, with the fact of being a fire and hence of essentially having the power to heat, while the second activity can be identified with the heat coming from fire and heating what is outside fire. In other words, the second activity is the effect of the inner activity of fire; it is the activity of fire in the external world.

According to Emilsson (2007, 60) we can identify six main characteristics of double activity: i) double activity is pervasive: it characterizes each level of the Plotinian universe, from the One to sensible realities; ii) the inner activity can be compared to a paradigm, while the external activity can be compared to a copy; iii) the double activity doctrine is described through emanative metaphors; iv) the external activity depends on the inner activity and cannot be separated from it: if the fire ceases, the heat that accompanied the fire will cease as well; v) the internal act is unaffected; vi) the internal act is also an active power. Most of these characteristics have antecedents in Platonic sources (see *Republic* VI.509b; *Timaeus* 29e; *Symposium* 212a–b; *Phaedrus* 245c–d; see also Gerson 1994, 24–25). Indeed, according to Emilsson, one can understand the doctrine of double *energeia* as the way in which Plotinus interprets the causality of intelligible realities in Plato and gives an account of Platonic causality from the viewpoint of the causes themselves (Emilsson 2007, 67). It is through the notion of double *energeia*, for example, that Plotinus explains how Intellect comes from the One, and how Soul comes from Intellect.

In our chapter, Plotinus refers to the *energeia* of the intelligible realm, but he does not specify how this *energeia* works for each intelligible level and he does not mention the activity or actuality of the One. Indeed, whether the One is beyond activity or does have an inner activity is a controversial issue. According to Dufour (2004, 200) and Horn (2002), Plotinus attributes only power to the One, but not activity or actuality, and this is precisely what distinguishes the One from Intellect, which is the first activity. Indeed, some passages might support this interpretation: in I.7.1, 19 and V.3.5, 36–38, Plotinus points out that the One transcends activity as it transcends being. However, in VI.8.20, we can find an explicit discussion of this issue, where the solution suggested is that the One is an activity without being: "Now certainly an activity not enslaved to substance is purely and simply free, and in this way he himself is himself from himself" (VI.8.20, 17–19). The difference between the One and Intellect, then, would be not that the One is beyond activity while Intellect is the first activity, but that, in the case of the One, activity is the act of the One's existence, but is not grounded in the One's essence. This reading enables us to apply the notion of double *energeia* to the relationship between the One and Intellect, where Intellect is to be identified with the One's second *energeia*, or, in other words, with the effect of the One's inner activity.

In addition to being crucial for Plotinus' account of the derivation from and ontological dependence upon the One of the whole of reality, the notion of *energeia* plays an important role in the description of the intelligible realm as a living totality. In V.3.7, Plotinus defines the being of Intellect as a self-directed activity. Not only does the Intellect eternally think itself, but even its content, the totality of Forms and individual intellects, is a self-directed activity of thinking. Indeed, for Plotinus the Forms are *noēseis*, acts of intellection or thoughts thinking themselves. This thinking activity is coupled with life. The last lines of chapter 3 conclude with a reference to the identification between this self-constituting and self-directed activity of the intelligible realities and life: everything in the intelligible realm is alive and is perfect life.

3, 22–25 *Is it in . . . compound in actuality*: At the end of chapter 2, Plotinus had defined actual being (*to energeiai*) as the compound of form and matter as distinguished from activity (*energeia*): *to energeiai* is the actuality of an existing thing that has been brought to actuality by something else. However, this definition of actual being cannot apply to intelligible realities, as it would imply that intelligible realities received their actuality from something else. This is why it is necessary to look for another meaning of actual being.

At lines 24 and 25, *hekaston* refers to intelligible reality. According to HS_2, *ho esti* at line 25 is an apposition to the subject: it could then be translated as "as to what it is," meaning that each intelligible reality is perfect in its own being. See also *ho esti* at line 34.

3, 27 *for in this . . . of another intellect*: If we were to assume that Intellect received its form instead of eternally having it, then we would need to pose another, prior, Intellect, responsible for bringing that Intellect from potentiality to actuality. We have seen, indeed, that potential being, contrary to power, needs something else already in actuality in order to be brought to actual being. We would then need a distinction between a passive and an active intellect, such as that posed by Aristotle for the individual soul in the short, and much discussed, passage of *On the Soul* 3.5.430a10–25. As we have seen, however, and in line with Aristotle's own view on this point, a state of passivity is not compatible with the nature of intelligible realities.

I take *nous* to be the subject of *deoito* at line 27.

3, 28 *On the contrary, the whole is within it*: That Intellect has everything within itself, namely all real beings or Forms, indicates its self-sufficiency and autarchy. On this, see for example V.1.4, 21–25: "But Intellect is all things. It has therefore everything at rest in the same place, and it only is, and its 'is' is for ever, and there is no place for the future, for then too it is—or for the past—for nothing there has passed away—but all things remain stationary forever, since they are the same, as if they were satisfied with themselves for being so" (translation: Armstrong).

3, 30 *this is activity*: Here, and at lines 31 and 33, I follow HS_1 and HS_2, instead of Kirchhoff: *energeia* and not *energeiai*. Indeed, as noted by Narbonne (1998, 54n71), "that which has itself from itself the fact of being always in such a way" is a description more appropriate to *activity* than to actual being.

3, 32 *the soul in the intelligible*: As pointed out by Blumenthal (1971), we can distinguish between three main levels concerning the soul: the hypostatic Soul or whole Soul, that remains always in the intelligible realm, eternally contemplating the Intellect from which it has been generated; the soul of the world, which organizes the cosmos into a living being, giving shape, life and order; and the individual souls. While all these levels are of a single nature, the life of the different levels is not the same. The soul of the world, indeed, is engaged not only in a contemplative activity, but also in organizing and governing the sensible realm. Contrary to the individual soul, however, the soul of the world is not affected in any way by the sensible realm and is eternally contemplating the intelligible reality above it. Hence, its activities are always the same. This is not the case for the individual soul, which, once descended into a body, engages in different activities and, while its real nature demands that it turn itself toward the intelligible realm, can get lost in the bodily life and forget its real origin. See IV.8.2, 31ff.; IV.8.3, 1ff.; IV.3.6.

The "Soul in the intelligible" refers then to the hypostatic Soul, which remains eternally turned toward Intellect, receiving from it the contents of its contemplation.

3, 34 *for example, the vegetative soul*: The vegetative soul (*hē phutikē*) is the lower soul, the nutritive faculty responsible for bodies' life and growth. The vegetative soul is a faculty of the soul of the world, which nurtures our individual bodies as well (see Blumenthal 1971, 26–28). The reason Plotinus claims that even the vegetative soul is an *energeia* is that, like all the other levels of the soul, the vegetative soul is an active power, and it is by being a power that it can nurture the bodies.

3, 35 *and are this way*: *kai houtōs* is understood by HS_2 as referring to the sensible realm: "etiam in mundo sensibili." Kirchhoff emends the text, suggesting to read *kai ontōs*, while Theiler deletes *kai houtōs* and supplements *oupō* later. According to HS_2, this difficult sentence indicates that Plotinus' opponent admits that everything is *energeiai* (in actuality), but asks whether everything should be considered as activity as well even in the sensible realm. The answer then would be negative: only intelligible realities are all both in actuality and activities.

An alternative reading might be that Plotinus' opponent here acknowledges that all intelligible realities are in actuality in the way Plotinus has just explained, namely without having been brought from potential to actual being in the way sensible compounds are; but he questions whether they should all be considered as activities as well. According to this reading, *houtōs* does not refer to the sensible realm, but rather to the description of the actual being of intelligible realities provided by Plotinus in the previous lines.

3, 36 *sleepless*: *agrupnos*. This line echoes Plato's *Timaeus* 52b7: *peri tēn aupnon kai alēthōs phusin*. This sleepless nature is the intelligible reality. See also *Ennead* VI.2.8, 7, concerning Intellect: *phōs en autōi aupnon*.

3, 37 *perfect life*: One can find a reference to *zōē aristē* in Aristotle's *Metaphysics*, 12.1072b26–28, where the activity of Intellect is defined as perfect life.

3, 38 *All [intelligible] realities . . . actuality and activity*: This chapter concludes by providing an answer to the opening questions of lines 2–3. We have, indeed, seen that each intelligible reality taken singularly as well as the intelligible realm taken as a whole are both in actuality and activity. This conclusion is accompanied by references to Plato's *Timaeus* and *Phaedrus* describing intelligible being as living and life.

3, 39 *the origin and source*: see *Phaedrus* 245c9.

3, 40 *true soul*: I follow HS_2 (*alēthous*) against Kirchhoff's emendation (*alēthōs*). True soul likely refers to the Soul in the intelligible realm, as distinguished from the soul in matter. See Narbonne (1998, 55n76).

Chapter 4

In this chapter Plotinus starts the examination of the case of prime matter. He first addresses the question raised at the beginning of chapter 2. A potential being is already a thing in actuality and is said to be in potentiality in relation to something else. Wood, for example, is potential in relation to the table, but it is already something in actuality, namely a piece of wood with a determinate size, color, texture, and so on. Plotinus' question is: does this apply also to the case of prime matter? Is prime matter, which is said to be potentially all realities, already some kind of being in actuality? He immediately rules out this hypothesis, for if matter were a tode ti, *a determinate thing in actuality, then it would be impossible for it to be all realities in potentiality. Indeed, absence of any form, quality, and quantity is the necessary prerequisite for it to be absolutely receptive. After having asserted this view, Plotinus starts drawing the consequences of it. Being in actuality and being are equivalent: in other words, it is impossible for something to be, except by being in actuality. Now, matter is neither a sensible being, because sensible beings that are, are also in actuality, nor is it an intelligible reality, since it certainly is not a form, but is rather formless. This means that matter is none of the beings, neither those that are generated upon it, nor those that are without matter. But being none of the beings means to be non-being: Plotinus will draw the consequences of this claim in the following and final chapter.*

4, 1–6 In order to be an actual thing, matter should already have a form and therefore be an individual substance. The lack of determination can be attributed, from two different points of view, both to prime matter and to proximate matter. In fact, proximate matter is also indeterminate in its relationship both to the form it will take in order to become actual and to the compound that accounts for its actual existence: for example, wood is indeterminate with regard both to the form of a table it will take and to the actual table itself. In *Metaphysics* 9.7.1049a27–36, Aristotle specifies that the subject, of which something is predicated, can be a *tode ti* or not, as the case may be: in the first instance, the subject or substrate is the individual substance, whereas, in the second, it is matter or the material substance and that which is predicated is a form. (An interesting discussion of form-matter predication as a not ordinary form of predication in this passage of *Metaphysics* can be found in Gill 2009, 391–427). See also *Metaphysics* 7.13.1038b4–6. In this second case, as far as its relationship to the form is concerned, the substrate can be considered as something indefinite and as the potential being of the new compound. This lack of determination, however, can be attributed to this substrate only within the context of a process of change, in which bronze as a potential statue becomes an actual statue. In other words, bronze is indefinite and indeterminate only from the point of view of its relationship either to the form that must be predicated of it in order for bronze to become a statue or to the compound, that is, the actual statue. Outside of this relationship, however, bronze is already a *tode ti*, a matter which is qualified in a certain way, and thus an actually existing thing.

Both in *Metaphysics* 9 and in *Physics* 3, the development of the theory of potential and actual being refers specifically to compounds, the individual substances and proximate matter, with respect to which the features and the conditions of potentiality are determined. These features and conditions, however, cannot be applied to the case of prime matter, which infringes both of the conditions quoted in the first chapter of our treatise: it is not already something in actuality and it is not potentially a particular thing, but is rather potentially all sensible realities. Now, there is a difference between being potentially something and being potentially everything or all realities. Even when in the material world a potential being is not actualized, it remains nevertheless something potential in its own direction, in which it *could* be actualized. For this reason, it has some kind of determination. But something that is potentially everything does not have any determination at all, even in its potential existence and in the direction in which it could be actualized (see Buchner 1970, 23).

The case of prime matter is therefore different from that of individual beings or of proximate matter. In *Metaphysics* 7.3.1029a20–21 Aristotle mentions the absolute lack of determination of matter, which is neither a something (*mēte ti*) nor a quantity (*mēte poson*), nor any of the categories (*mēte allo mēden legetai hois hōristai to on*). The nature and the very existence of prime matter in Aristotle's thought is a problematic issue that goes much beyond the scope of this commentary. In his very detailed work, Happ pointed out the presence of at least two different conceptions of prime matter in Aristotle: a completely indeterminate and only conceptual matter, "Hyle-Prinzip," conceived of as general substrate, and a concrete corporeal quantitatively determined matter of the physical world, prime matter itself (see Happ 1971, 696ff.). For a discussion of Happ's position and of the debate on Aristotelian prime matter, see Narbonne (1993, 237–249).

Regardless of whether Aristotle conceived of a prime matter or not, in *On Aristotle's Metaphysics* 292.25, commenting on *Metaphysics* 4.4.1007b26, Alexander of Aphrodisias points out, as regards matter, that it is indeterminate (*aoristos*), being potentially all realities (*dunamei panta*) and therefore actually none of them (*energeiai de mēden*). The use of the expression *dunamei panta* is a clear indication of the fact that Alexander is referring to prime matter and not to proximate matter, which certainly could not be potentially all realities: wool, for example, is certainly not potentially a saw. And, indeed, Alexander, commenting on Book 5 of *Metaphysics*, stresses that prime matter, in contrast to proximate matter, does not have an actual existence (*On Aristotle's Metaphysics* 358.37–359.11). Whereas the proximate matter of everything is an individual actual body, prime matter considered in itself is nothing akin to an individual thing. In *On Aristotle's Metaphysics* 291.25, we can find the definition of prime matter as non-being—the obvious consequence of the fact that it is not an actual thing—a definition that Plotinus develops, as we will see, but in a manner that neither Aristotle nor Alexander would have accepted.

This brief survey shows that Plotinus was already able to find in the Peripatetic tradition the notion of a prime matter as potentiality of everything and as nothing in actuality.

4, 3 *which is said to exist*: As we will discover a few lines below, matter is improperly said to be, since properly speaking it is other than being.

4, 4 *potentially everything*: Narbonne has stressed the fact that we cannot find a definition of matter as *panta dunamei* in Aristotle (see Narbonne 1998, 56n79). As we have seen, however, the source of this definition could be Alexander of Aphrodisias, *On Aristotle's Metaphysics* 292.25. By defining matter as potentially all realities, Plotinus is not distancing himself from the Aristotelian tradition.

4, 5–6 *For in this . . . be potentially everything*: In order to be entirely receptive, matter cannot have any form, quality, or quantity, and therefore it cannot be an actual being. Plotinus had already partially exposed his theory of matter in *Ennead* II.4. His starting point in this treatise (*Enn.* II.4. 1, 1) is the terminological conflation between the Aristotelian notion of *hupokeimenon* in *Physics* 1.9.192a31 and the Platonic view of *chōra* as the receptacle (*hupodochē*) of the Forms in *Timaeus* 49a6. Plato's receptacle and Aristotle's *hulē* as *hupokeimenon* were in all likelihood being equated already within Plato's Academy itself at a rather early stage (see Aristotle, *Physics* 4.2.209b–210a, and Fleet 2012, 167). The *Timaeus*, indeed, was the source of two rather different accounts of matter: one, which became commonly accepted by different philosophical schools, elaborated on a notion of matter as material substrate, and lost the entirely negative character of Plato's receptacle; the second, supported by Plotinus, interpreted the *Timaeus* more literally, maintaining the identification between matter and privation, and therefore the absolutely negative character of matter (see Fleet 2012, 169).

In Plotinus' view, in order to be the receptacle of all forms, matter needs to be simple, continuous, without quality, and without quantity. Since the function of the forms is to give order, limits, and determinacy, we need to suppose the existence of something the function of which is to receive order, limits, and determination: hence we need the concept of a receptacle that is both *aoristos* and *apeiros*, indeterminate and unlimited. This is why Plotinus insists, in II.4.15, that matter does not have limitlessness by accident, since limitlessness is not a *logos* that can be predicated of something. Matter is rather limitlessness in itself. Absence of form implies also an absence of extension: Plotinus is careful in stressing that matter is not a receptacle in the way a vessel, already with a certain volume and a certain size, would be. In II.4.11 he underlines the fact that we have a tendency to wrongly attribute a volume or a mass to matter. The reason for this is that the first representation of matter we have, a representation that could be defined as unreflective and based on imagination, depicts it as a volume (*onkos*). When we try to imagine or think about matter, we cannot avoid making it spatial. A second reason for this wrong attribution lies in the fact that matter has some kind of predisposition to volume, that is to say, volume is the first thing that matter receives (II.4.11, 27–29). In the context of a discussion on potentiality and actuality, the definition of matter as limitlessness, indeterminacy, and absolute receptivity is equivalent to excluding the possibility that matter can be something in actuality, for being in actuality precisely implies having a limit, a determination, and therefore a limited, determinate potentiality.

4, 6–18 In the rest of the chapter Plotinus addresses the consequence of the impossibility for matter to be something in actuality: matter is non-being (*mē on*). Matter is defined as non-being first in relation to sensible things that are generated upon it (lines 6–8), second in relation to intelligible beings, which are not compounds of matter and form, but are pure forms (lines 10–13).

4, 8 *none of those . . . generated upon it*: The beings generated upon matter are sensible realities, compounds of matter and form. The expression "upon matter," *ep'autēs*, emphasizes the fact that compounds are generated due to the imposition of forms upon a formless matter. As Plotinus will explain in III.6.14, these compounds are like reflections projected upon matter as upon a mirror. In this treatise Plotinus expressly denies that matter constitutes a real compound together with the form. To show the way in which matter and form remain mutually unconnected, Plotinus resorts, amongst other arguments, to the simile of the mirror: the *logoi* are projected by the Soul on matter, being reflected upon it as if upon a mirror, without altering it, modifying it and joining with it in a compound. The image of the mirror is intended to convey both the mutual extraneousness of matter and form and the fleetingness and ontological weakness of the images reflected on the mirror, namely the sensible objects. The sensible objects are nothing but *eidōla*, simulacra, constantly changing, totally dependent on the superior intelligible reality. To describe this particular relationship between matter and form, Igal (1982, 68) and Linguiti (2007, 105–122) suggest the notion of "pseudo-hylomorphism." If hylomorphism indicates a real union of matter and form in the constitution of a sensible object, it is exactly this kind of union of matter and form in a compound that Plotinus denies in the material world, even though he keeps asserting the necessity of matter for the existence of sensible bodies. The term "pseudo-hylomorphism" fulfils various functions: on the one hand, it accounts for the fact that, in the *Enneads*, we often find a terminology that draws on hylomorphic conceptions, which assert the presence of a material and of a formal aspect in a sensible object; on the other hand, however, it highlights the deceptiveness of this terminology, for Plotinus denies that matter actually partakes in the constitution of the sensible objects (see Wildberg 2009, and Chiaradonna 2008). From this point of view, not only is there no real unity of matter and form within the sensible objects, but it is also likely that in the *Enneads* the very notion of proximate matter is absent, because proximate matter would require real hylomorphism.

While matter does not enter into a real hylomorphic unity with the form in the compound, it is still necessary for the production of sensible objects. In II.4.11 Plotinus asserts that the intelligible qualities alone would not have been sufficient for the constitution of bodies: without a receptacle ready to receive them and, as he specifies in the following chapter, without the contribution of matter, the *logoi* would have remained rational principles and would not have become bodies. He refutes therefore the hypothesis that bodies can be the product of a mere union of intelligible forms or formative principles, since in this case it would be missing an element able to give birth to three-dimensional volume, without being volume itself. If the *logoi* alone cannot account for the existence of the sensible reality, matter, as the Platonic receptacle, represents at least the condition of its production, of its existence, and of its ontological difference from intelligible reality. In III.6.15–18, Plotinus stresses that, even though it cannot be identified with place, space, or size, matter provides Nature with the possibility to create a space and for the *logoi* to become spatial. Matter represents the condition for the existence of the *logoi* in space, but it is not itself spatial and does not partake in the sensible compound, since, as we will see in chapter 5, it is impassible, unchangeable, and bound to remain only potential.

4, 9–10 *if it is true . . . generated upon matter*: Plotinus has shown that matter cannot be any of the sensible realities, because these are actual beings. Here he addresses a possible objection: the fact that matter is none of the sensible beings is not sufficient to define matter as non-being, since there are realities that are not sensible and are not compounds of matter and form. Could matter not be one of those? This question equates to asking whether matter is an intelligible reality.

4, 12 *imagined*: It is not by chance that Plotinus uses the word *phantazomenē*. Indeed, in virtue of its complete absence of form, matter is absolute indeterminacy and limitlessness, and therefore cannot be grasped either by intellection or by discursive reasoning: on the contrary, indeterminacy can be grasped only through the indeterminate, according to the principle that the similar is known by the similar. The only possible reasoning about what is indeterminate and unlimited in itself will therefore be the *nothos logismos*, the spurious reasoning mentioned by Plato in *Timaeus* 52b2 (see II.4.10, 11). In other words, matter cannot be a proper object of thought, hence we cannot have any clear concept of it, but only a vague image.

4, 12–13 *hence it cannot . . . the intelligibles either*: The hypothesis that matter is an intelligible reality is quickly ruled out: intelligible realities are forms, whereas matter is imagined (*phantazomenē*) as formless. *Ekei* and *ekeina* are expressions that Plotinus typically employs to refer to the intelligible world and the intelligible realities. *Ekeinois* at line 13 is opposed to *tauta* at line 11, which indicates sensible realities. For the Greek text, I follow Kirchhoff and HS_2 (*an* *arithmētheiē*), and not HS_1 (*on arithmētheiē*), which reports the text as found in manuscript A_I , manuscript family x, and manuscript Q.

4, 16 *those that are falsely said to be*: Sensible beings are defined as false beings in opposition to the true beings, which are the intelligible realities. Indeed, Plotinus strongly criticizes the Aristotelian application of the category of substance to sensible objects (see, for example VI.3.8). The so-called "sensible substance" is a mere aggregation of matter and qualities, which, not being able to find its essential principle in itself, must necessarily find it in something else, namely in the intelligible *logoi*, on which it depends ontologically. Consistently, in VI.3.15, Plotinus states that the so-called "sensible substance" must rather be considered as a "qualified" than as a "something." Each sensible object depends on an intelligible *logos*, which is not only the rational model, but also the organizing and producing active principle that sets up the multiplicity of qualities constituting the sensible object in a coherent whole and guarantees the self-identity of the latter (see Kalligas 1997, 401 and Kalligas 2011).

4, 17 *an image of a rational principle*: The idea that sensible realities are copies of the intelligible Forms is fully articulated by Plato in *Timaeus* 27d–29d, where Timaeus defines the sensible cosmos as an *eikōn* of the intelligible patterns. The word *indalma*, as well as the word *eidōlon*, appearance or image, which Plotinus often uses in relation to sensible objects, express the phantom-like nature of sensible objects. Although sensible realities are only an image of the intelligible world, they still participate in it, for they are compounds of matter and of a form coming from rational principles. Matter, on the contrary, does not participate in the Forms, and therefore it is not even an image of the intelligible reality the way sensible objects are. Plotinus will insist on the relation of similarity between the intelligible realm and the physical universe in II.9 [33], in his polemics against the Gnostic depreciation of the sensible world.

Chapter 5

In this last chapter, Plotinus restates the conclusion reached in the previous chapter. There we had seen that the two Aristotelian theses set out in lines 10–21 of the first chapter, namely that something potential is already something else in actuality, and that something is always potential in a qualified way, do not hold in the case of prime matter. Indeed, prime matter is neither already something in actuality nor is it potentially a particular thing, because it is rather potentially all realities. Thereafter, Plotinus draws the consequences of this conclusion. In lines 10–19 he revises the third Aristotelian thesis expounded in 1, 10–21, namely that something is potential if it can be actualized. In other words, in order to say that something is in potentiality something else, there must be the possibility, under given circumstances, for this thing to be actualized. According to Plotinus, if matter is nothing in actuality and everything in potentiality, it follows for the same reasons that it cannot be actualized. Although it is in potentiality, prime matter cannot and will not be actualized and therefore will not become something else. Here

Plotinus decidedly differentiates himself from Aristotle and the Aristotelian tradition. This consideration compels Plotinus to address further the peculiar nature of matter, which he had already defined as non-being in the previous chapter.

5, 1–10 In these lines Plotinus restates the conclusions already reached in chapter 4. Matter is nothing in actuality and is everything in potentiality. If matter were something in actuality, it would not be prime matter, but rather proximate matter, in the same way bronze is (line 9). Being in actuality would imply that matter already has a set of qualities that make it predisposed to be the matter of a specific set of objects. For example, bronze can be the matter of a statue, a door, a gate, but it cannot be the matter of an edible pudding. The consequence of this is that matter cannot be everything in potentiality, but rather only some specific things. Thus it is necessary to insist on the absolute lack of actuality of prime matter.

5, 2–3 *So then, insofar . . . is going to be*: In the previous line, Plotinus had stated that matter is the matter of everything by being in potentiality. Now the question arises whether being in potentiality for matter entails having some qualities that predispose it to what it is going to be. For example, the qualities that iron possesses predispose it to be the proximate matter of objects such as saws, knives, locks, etc., while they do not predispose it to become a notebook or a box of matches. In addition to this, according to the Aristotelian doctrine of potentiality, it is precisely because a being has determinate properties that it can be said to be potentially something.

5, 3 *But being for it is only a promise*: *alla* has an adversative function and, as Denniston notes, can be used within a hypophora (i.e., a question or objection that the speaker or author asks himself) in order to introduce the reply (see Denniston 1954, 10). Plotinus rejects the possibility that matter has any property in accordance with the realities that are going to be: matter is in potentiality a mere vague promise of the future. As he states in the following line, the being of matter lies only in what will come to be, for in itself matter has no being.

5, 8 *therefore, it would . . . in every way*: *Pantē hulē*, literally "wholly matter" or "entirely matter," is the expression Plotinus is using in order to refer to prime matter. The precondition for something to be prime matter is to be completely deprived of any quality. The difference between prime matter and proximate matter is, indeed, that only the first, in virtue of its absolute absence of any quality, can be everything in potentiality, while the second, for example bronze, can be only a set of things in potentiality.

5, 9–10 *Matter is therefore . . . being," as movement*: Plotinus reintroduces the identification between matter and non-being, with reference to Plato's *Sophist* 256d5–6. In order to understand what Plotinus has in mind when he defines matter as non-being, we need to briefly address his interpretation of otherness in the *Sophist*. In this dialogue Plato elaborates on a notion of non-being as otherness, to be distinguished from the Parmenidean absolute nothingness: otherness is one of the five great genera, together with being, sameness, movement, and rest. By participating in otherness, the other genera are other than being (for example, the genus movement is other than the genus being), and therefore, in a sense, they are non-being (for by saying that movement is other than being, one says by the same token that movement is not being) (*Sophist* 256d–256e). Indeed, in order to have reciprocal relations between the various genera, we need the concept of a non-being that in a sense is, namely otherness. It is through otherness that, for example, movement excludes rest, as movement needs to participate in otherness in order not to be rest: "That's because as applied to all of them the nature of *the different* makes each of them not be, by making it different from that which is. And we're going to be right if we say that all of them *are not* in this same way. And on the other hand we're also going to be right if we call them beings, because they have a share in that which is" (*Sophist* 256d12–e4, translation: White).

Otherness, however, albeit a kind of non-being, is not the absolute non-being of which Parmenides claimed it is impossible to speak. This is why it is a non-being that is. This notion of otherness alone would not be sufficient to grasp the meaning of Plotinus' identification of matter with non-being. However, after having shown the necessity of otherness, the protagonist of the *Sophist*, the Eleatic Stranger, suggests comparing the nature of otherness to knowledge, which, while being a single thing, has many parts, each of which applies to a different object and has a proper name. The same happens with the nature of otherness, as different parts of otherness apply to different objects in order to negate them (*Sophist* 257c–d13): "The nature of the different appears to be chopped up, just like knowledge." For example, there is a part of otherness that applies to the beautiful, and this part will be called "non-beautiful." In the same way, we will have a "non-just," a "non-good," and of course also a "non-being." The Stranger had previously explained that otherness should not be conflated with contrariety. To say that something is "non-beautiful," then, does not mean to say that it is ugly (on this point see Dixsaut 1991).

According to the reading of this complex passage offered by Lee, the nature of the parts of otherness that apply to various objects consists solely of their non-being. In other words, the "part of otherness" is an intensional, not an extensional, determination of otherness in relation to a determinate X. When I say non-beautiful, I am not indicating the set of all Forms that are not the Form of the beautiful, nor am I indicating a specific set of Forms incompatible with the Form of the beautiful. On the contrary, the negation "non-beautiful" has only an intensional meaning, and this meaning is nothing but the exclusion of the term that I am negating, namely the beautiful (see Lee 1972).

To summarize, the *Sophist* provides us with two kinds of non-being not to be identified with absolute nothingness. On the one hand, we have the genus otherness, which is otherness in itself or absolute otherness, and which is the contrary of the genus sameness. On the other hand, we have the part of otherness that negates being, both being in general and the being of each determinate object. The content of this second kind of non-being is nothing but the negation of being (*Sophist* 258a–c).

Coming back to Plotinus' reading of the *Sophist*, we can find a reference to the part of otherness which is opposed to being in II.4.16, 1–3: "Is matter, then, the same thing as otherness? No, rather it is the same thing as the part of otherness which is opposed to the things which in the full and proper sense exist, that is to say rational formative principles" (translation: Armstrong). Here, Plotinus clarifies that we should identify matter not with the Form of otherness, but rather with the part of otherness that negates the *logoi*. This is confirmed by a passage from a much later treatise, I.8 [51], which shows some resemblance with II.5.5, 9–10, and can help shed light on the identification between matter and non-being. In I.8.3, 6–9, Plotinus, speaking of matter as non-being, clarifies: "Non-being here does not mean absolute non-being but only something other than being; not non-being in the same way as the movement and the rest which affect being, but like an image of being or something still more non-existent" (translation: Armstrong).

In this passage, we find three different notions of non-being: absolute non-being, non-being as the genus otherness, and non-being as the part of otherness that negates being. Plotinus attributes to matter the third form of non-being: matter is other than being in the sense of a lack of participation in being, in the same way in which non-beautiful expresses simply a lack of participation in the beautiful. We see therefore that matter does not have any content but its lack of any participation in being, which is *not* equivalent to absolute nothingness.

To these three kinds of non-being we need to add the specific non-being of the One, which is beyond and superior to being: VI.9.2, 46–47 (see Narbonne 1992).

5, 10–23 In these lines, Plotinus challenges one of the three Aristotelian theses mentioned in chapter 1, namely that something is in potentiality if it is capable of change. Does this view hold for prime matter as well? Since Aristotle barely speaks of prime matter, we must turn to Alexander of Aphrodisias. In *On Aristotle's Metaphysics* 291.25ff., Alexander points out, against Anaxagoras, the merely potential nature of matter, for matter *cannot* be the actual totality of things. The fact of being potentially all realities does not have a corresponding actual existence as the simultaneous totality of things and, in this sense, matter can only be and must remain potential. Matter, however, *can* change into *each one* of the things which derive from it. Even though prime matter considered in itself, *qua* matter, is only potential, it is the substrate *out of which* material bodies are constituted and therefore it partakes in the process of change which produces the compounds of matter and form. The fact that matter changes when it receives the forms is also explicitly asserted by Alexander as quoted by Simplicius: *Commentary on the Physics* 320.20–26, and in *Questions (Quaestiones)* 1.24.38, 1–14. In other words, matter can be transformed and, indeed, we cannot find any matter existing only *qua* matter, separated from form and therefore unchanged. It is exactly because of the fact that matter does not have a separate existence that it cannot be the right candidate for substance in a strong sense, as Aristotle explains in *Metaphysics* 7.1029a27–28.

The Plotinian perspective is radically different. Plotinus, indeed, specifies that matter is unable to transform itself (lines 12–13). Imprisoned between two kinds of being, intelligible and sensible (lines 19–20), matter does not succeed in becoming either in actuality. These lines might be better understood in the light of treatise III.6 [26], in which Plotinus deals with the question of the impassibility of bodiless realities. Here, after having argued in favor of the impassibility of the soul in the first five chapters, Plotinus develops throughout the remaining 14 chapters the issue of the impassibility and immutability of prime matter. The question raised at the beginning of this examination (III.6.6, 3–5) as to whether we must think that matter is subject to affections or not, problematizes the definition proposed in II.5.1, 29–31 of potential existence as substrate of affections, forms, and shapes. What needs to be analyzed, in fact, is in what sense we can assert that matter is a substrate, especially if we take into account the arguments developed in chapters 4 and 5 of II.5, according to which matter is the bare potentiality of all realities and is not able to be actualized. Even though, in III.6, Plotinus still uses the Aristotelian terms of *hulē* and *hupokeimenon*, the conclusions are radically anti-Aristotelian, whereas the explicit references to the *Timaeus* and to the Platonic theory of the unchangeable receptacle abound: see, for example III.6.7, 27–28 (*Timaeus* 50c4–5); 8, 11–12 (*Timaeus* 52a8–b1); 10, 9 (*Timaeus* 51a7); 11, 1–5 (*Timaeus* 50c4–5). Prime matter is impassible, it is subject neither to alteration nor to corruption, and it does not give birth to a unitary compound together with the form (see III.6.12, 1–4). The main reason that impels Plotinus to assert the impassibility of matter is extensively explained in chapter 10: if matter were subject to the affections and really received the forms, changing itself, we would no longer have a receptive subject or substrate empty of qualities, size, measure, and all determination able to receive the multiplicity of forms. Instead, we would have an already qualified subject, whose qualities would unavoidably interact with the *logoi* that are projected onto it. In this way, matter would not be universally receptive (*pandeches*) any longer; and, indeed, it would be subject to corruption. From this explanation one can also see a critique of Alexander's position, according to which prime matter is at the same time the potentiality of all realities and is able to become separately each one of them, therefore taking part in the process of becoming. In other words, how is it possible to continue to assert that prime matter is potentially all realities once it has lost its essential feature, the absolute lack of determination? The only solution to this problem lies in taking up again the Platonic theory of the unchangeable receptacle, combined with the Peripatetic theory of the substrate as the potentiality of all realities. Matter must remain external to the process of becoming, must stand as an irreducible otherness, in order to play the role of permanent substrate.

As far as the notion of the impassibility of matter is concerned, the theory of the prime substrate appears radically modified in Plotinus with regard to the Peripatetic tradition. The substrate is no longer the matter *ex hēs*, out of which bodies are constituted—it is only a receptacle in and from which the *logoi* enter and emerge, which does not put up any resistance to this alternation of forms that come and go as if passing through water (III.6.7, 31–33). For this definition, Plotinus largely resorts to the Platonic vocabulary of the *Timaeus*: matter is receptacle (*hē hupodochē*) and wet-nurse of every becoming (*tithēnē geneseōs*), it is space (*chōra*) and seat (*hedra*) (III.6.13, 12–18 and *Timaeus* 49a5–6e; 52a8–b1). It does not transmit anything to what is generated and this is why it is called "mother" by those who assert that the mother does not contribute anything to the nature of the unborn baby and, inasmuch as she is absolutely sterile and impotent, confines herself only to receiving (III.6.19, 19–25). Affections, alterations, and changes concern bodies with quantity and size, and not prime matter. The way matter receives the forms without actually receiving them and participates in them without participating is the subject of a long explanation developed in chapter 11, once again on the basis of Plato's *Timaeus*: that is, a non-participating participation which leaves matter in a condition of eternal need, like Penia in Plato's *Symposium*, who is only capable of covering herself with cunning appearances (III.6.14, 5–18). Plotinus therefore solves in a radical way the question that was already raised in the last chapters of II.5. If one wants to argue coherently that prime matter is the substrate of every sensible being and of becoming, the only coherent candidate for this role is a substrate that functions as an unchangeable receptacle, following the Platonic notion of a receptacle that not only is not actually something, but can never become anything actual and must therefore permanently remain a bare potential existence, the existence of non-being. It is on this particular point that the difference between Plotinus and the Peripatetic tradition can be seen.

Corrigan (1996, 111–116 and 129–130) correctly stresses that Plotinus was already able to find in Alexander of Aphrodisias the terms of a notion of matter as *dunamei panta* and deftly points out Alexander's view according to which matter is *not yet* actually the things it can become. This statement would be very close to Plotinus' assertions about the potential being of matter. However, saying that matter is *not yet* the actual compounds does not imply any impossibility with regard to its actualization. On the contrary, Plotinus performs a radical gesture, cutting off, as far as prime matter is concerned, the correspondence between potential and actual existence. In this way, he elaborates the notion of a potentiality which is bound to remain non-actualized, the exact contrary of what Aristotle argues in *Metaphysics* 9.3.1047a24–28. In the latter text, Aristotle states that a thing is called potential (or possible) if its actualization does not imply any impossibility. In other words, in order to say that a thing is potentially something, this thing must be able to be actualized when the necessary conditions for its actualization are given, without coming up against any constitutive impossibility. A potential existence is not characterized by the necessity of its actualization, but at least by its effective possibility. Now, according to Plotinus, the case of prime matter seems precisely to contradict this condition. Prime matter, in fact, is potentially all realities, but its actualization is prevented by an absolute impossibility of transformation. What is projected onto it as a *phantasma* is not the actualization of its potentiality, but exclusively the active potentiality of the *logoi*. The potentiality of matter therefore does not have any relationship to the actual existence of sensible objects. It is a very special kind of potentiality, which serves to define a very special kind of existence, the existence of matter, the existence of a simulacrum (lines 22–23), which is an allusion to what will come to be and a real lie (*alēthinōs pseudos*) (lines 23–24).

5, 11–12 *reject, entirely separated*: In a previous treatise, *Ennead* IV.8 [6] 6, 18–23, Plotinus suggests that matter does participate in the intelligible and is not isolated: "If, then, the nature of matter always existed, it was impossible for it not to participate, because of its very existence, in that which bestows the good on everything to the extent that each thing can receive it. Or else, if the coming to be of matter was a necessary consequence of prior causes, not even in this case did it need to exist in isolation as if that which grants being like some favor had come to a halt before reaching it because of some inability" (translation: Fleet). While in this treatise Plotinus denies that matter exists in isolation (*chōris*), in II.5.5, 11–12 he insists that matter is entirely separated (*chōristheisa*). The notion of matter's isolation can also be found in III.6.9, 37–38, where Plotinus, referring to Plato's *Philebus* 63b7–8, writes that matter, contrary to the compound, is impassible, for it is isolated from the other beings (*erēmon tōn allōn*) and simple, non-mixed (*haploun*). Similar terms (*chōris; kechōrismena; kechōristai*) recur in a much later treatise, I.8, where Plotinus, challenging Aristotle's idea that the contraries must have a genus or a species in common, explains that matter is the contrary of the One in virtue of its complete separation from it. Matter is the contrary of the One, and therefore evil, precisely because it does not have anything in common with the One: I.8.6, 38; 54; 58. This passage, therefore, seems to exclude any form of participation of matter in the intelligible, since not having anything in common with the One means not having any unity, and—except for the One—unity is coextensive with being.

Fleet (2012, 169–172), commenting on IV.8.6, 18–23, correctly suggests that matter should not be identified with pure non-being, with what is not in any way at all, for it has an essential role in the generation of the sensible world. But he also insists that matter can participate. This latter claim should be taken with some caution, especially considering that Plotinus seems to exclude any participation in later treatises. Narbonne (1998, 59n99) suggests a developmentalist approach in order to solve the contradiction between the passage in IV.8, and the insistence on the separation of matter in later treatises. However, we can avoid a developmentalist solution to the apparent inconsistency between these passages by paying attention to their different contexts. In IV.8, Plotinus is dealing not with matter and its nature, but rather with the problem of the descent of the soul into bodies. Matter is therefore addressed from the viewpoint of the task proper to the soul. This task consists of not leaving anything without an enlightenment coming from above, for the good cannot remain jealously within itself. This is why the soul must give something to matter, by projecting the *logoi* upon it and giving birth in this way to the great beauty of the sensible world. This passage, therefore, does not say anything about the nature of matter or the capacity of matter to participate. While Plotinus writes that matter has a share, having a share should be understood just as a description of the operation of the soul giving a gift to matter. What we do not know from this text is whether matter is capable of receiving this gift or not.

The passages in II.5, III.6, and I.8, on the contrary, do not deal with the operations of the soul, but rather with the nature of matter itself: the viewpoint is completely different. Now, while the soul does project the *logoi* upon matter, in order for the good to be diffused, matter remains separated. This separation should be understood as referring to the incapacity of matter both to turn toward what is above and to receive a form. In this case, therefore, we have an indication concerning the very nature of matter, which is separated because of its own incapacity to participate, and not because it was rejected by the intelligible realities above it. Indeed, matter is the only outcome of the procession that does not have any desire, and therefore it does not have any longing (*orexis*) for the Good (see, for example, VI.7.28). If we take into account the different perspectives in these treatises, we can make perfect sense of what Plotinus is saying and resolve any apparent inconsistency.

To summarize, from the viewpoint of the soul matter participates, because the soul projects the *logoi* upon it. From the viewpoint of the nature of matter, matter does not participate, because it is incapable of turning towards the soul and being formed.

5, 17–18 *appearing once the . . . have left off*: These lines are among the few passages in the entire *Enneads* that refer to the generation of matter, albeit in a rather unclear way. As a consequence of the ambiguity and unclarity that characterize all the passages concerning the generation of matter, scholars have suggested an array of different interpretive options. Is matter generated or not? Is it generated in time or eternally generated? And what generates matter and how? In the last decade the thesis defended by Denis O'Brien (1991), according to which matter is eternally generated by the lower soul, has been largely accepted. Indeed, we can find in several treatises allusions to the fact that the soul generates or ought to generate something after itself. See, for example, V.1.7, 43–48; III.9.3, 7–12; III.9.3, 7–12; and III.4.1, 5–12, which is the most explicit passage on this subject.

Lines 7–18 mention the fact that matter appears when the intelligible realities have ended. This is consistent with what we learn from I.8.7, 16–23: "One can grasp the necessity of evil in this way too. Since not only the Good exists, there must be the last end to the process of going out past it, or if one prefers to put it like this, going down or going away: and this last, after which nothing else can come into being, is evil. Now it is necessary that what comes after the First should exist, and therefore that the Last should exist; and this is matter, which possesses nothing at all of the Good. And in this way too evil is necessary" (translation: Armstrong). In I.8 we find the most extensive treatment not only of evil but also of the identification between absolute evil and prime matter. One of the reasons provided by Plotinus for the necessary existence of evil is precisely the fact that once we have a series of realities generated starting from the One, this series cannot go on endlessly. Matter/evil is, therefore, the end and the last element of the series: it is last because—contrary to the Intellect and the Soul, which are generated as indeterminate, but which have the capacity both of turning themselves toward their origin in order to receive determination and of producing something else after themselves—matter has no capacities at all. Being absolutely powerless, not only can it not turn itself toward the soul that generated it, but it cannot generate something else after itself either. In matter, then, the generative power which characterizes intelligible realities is exhausted, and this is why matter is what remains when the intelligible beings have left off.

Two alternative views on the generation of matter have been offered by Corrigan (1986) and Narbonne (1998, 122–136; 2006; 2007). The first suggests that in the *Enneads* there is not just one generation of matter, but rather multiple generations of multiple matters. The second challenges O'Brien's conclusion that matter is generated by the soul, and suggests a different model of generation. When the One generates the Intellect, the first outcome of this generation is the so-called inchoative intellect, or intelligible otherness, or indeterminate intellect. According to Narbonne, a part of this intelligible otherness "flees," without any contribution of the hypostases. This flight of indeterminacy is not immanent to the procession; this is why matter finds its place at the end of the whole reality, and is eternally separated and absolutely other. Narbonne's identification of the generation of matter with a "flight" from the intelligible otherness is based on a reading of II.4.5, 20–28; II.5.4, 14–18 and 5, 9–22, where Plotinus speaks of a "fleeing matter." While Narbonne is right in noting that the passages that seem to suggest a generation of matter by the soul are rather obscure and ambiguous, his own solution to the problem raises more problems than it was meant to solve. Indeed, the notion of an uncontrolled flight that would take place within the intelligible reality and that would not be part of the procession introduces within the intelligible realm an element of contingency incompatible with the necessary character of the hierarchical generation of beings among the intelligibles.

5, 18–19 *and being caught . . . place among them*: As we have already seen, matter contributes to the existence of sensible objects only insofar as it is the entirely passive mirror that allows the *logoi* to become spatialized, tridimensional. As matter is not generative at all, the only generative cause in the constitution of sensible reality is the soul, while matter is only a condition for their appearance. This is the reason why matter is inferior even to sensible realities, for these take part in the *logoi* coming from the soul and in its generative power, while matter does not. Matter is, therefore, last not only in relation to intelligible realities, but also in relation to sensible beings.

5, 23–36 The conclusion of the treatise is articulated as a progression of metaphorical, oxymoronic expressions, quotations from Plato's dialogues, and suggestive definitions of the peculiar being of matter. "Phantasm in actuality," "lie in actuality," "true lie," "real non-being": Plotinus multiplies the labels in a breathtaking succession of terms as each of them is inadequate to grasp the elusive and faint being of matter. More than an existing thing, matter is the shadow of an existence, or rather the aspiration to existence (*hupostaseōs ephesis*), as suggestively indicated in III.6.7, 13. Indeed, the being of matter is only in relation to what will come to be, it consists of its being potentially everything, of its announcing what is going to be. There is nothing left outside this relational tension toward what will appear on its surface as on a mirror. If the essence of matter is identical to its being potential, being transformed and actualized for matter would entail the destruction of its very essence, and therefore of its existence (lines 30–33).

In III.6.14, 14–17, this projection toward what will come to be is expressed through the resort to the image of Penia from Plato's *Symposium* 203b–204a: Plotinus, indeed, identifies matter with Penia, absolute poverty, a never satisfied striving, which covers itself with ingenious appearances. The description of matter as absolute poverty is consistent with its identification with absolute privation, which is fully articulated in II.4. Here Plotinus insists, against Aristotle, on the identification between *hulē* and *sterēsis*, denying that privation can be attributed to matter as if it were a quality or a predicate (II.4.13, 20–23). According to Aristotle, substrate and privation must be distinguished as the substrate and the accident (*Physics* 1.6.189b–9.192b). In other words, privation is only accidentally predicated of the substrate. Indeed, matter is the substrate which is deprived of qualities, but which can, through a process of change and actualization, acquire these qualities it was deprived of: bronze, for example, is accidentally the privation of the form of the statue, but it does acquire that form when it is shaped by a sculptor. This is why matter cannot be identified with privation: otherwise we would have to admit that the substrate is destroyed whenever it goes through a process of change in which it receives the qualities that it did not have before the change, that is, whenever it ceases to be the privation of those qualities. For example, if we identify the bronze with privation, then we must say that the bronze gets destroyed when it is transformed into a bronze statue.

Against Aristotle, Plotinus insists that if privation were a quality predicated of matter, then matter would not be absolutely deprived of qualities, but would be qualified. In this case, as we have already seen, matter could not play the role of the general substrate. Privation, however, cannot be a quality, for it is a negation, and precisely because privation is a negation, the definition of matter and that of privation cannot be distinguished: therefore, they are the same (II.4.14). The problem raised by Aristotle finds a solution in Plotinus' pseudo-hylomorphism. Matter *qua* privation cannot be destroyed through a process of change because matter does not undergo any change at all, it cannot be destroyed by receiving the qualities it was the privation of, because it cannot receive any quality or shape or form at all. Matter remains poverty and privation without any possibility of being transformed, actualized, or fulfilled.

5, 22 *So, it is a phantasm in actuality*: The expression *energeiai eidōlon* and the following expression *energeiai pseudos*, "a lie in actuality," convey the idea that matter is only potential, but from another viewpoint. Being only potential, matter is privation and non-being. At the same time, the non-being of matter should not be conflated with the Parmenidean absolute nothingness of which it is impossible to speak. Matter does have some tenuous, faint form of existence, but it is a false existence, the existence of a phantasm or mere appearance without ontological consistency, unity or stability.

5, 23–24 *This is the . . . a "true lie"*: *alēthinōs pseudos*, see Plato, *Republic* 382a4. The somewhat oxymoronic expression "true lie," *alēthōs peudos*, appears in Plato's *Republic* within the discussion about poetry and education in Book III. Here Socrates distinguishes between two different kinds of lie: the lie in words, which does not necessarily correspond to a deception of the soul, as in the case of tales that are false but that convey some true moral content; and the lie in the soul, the "true lie," which entails the deception or self-deception of the soul, and in particular of reason. Plotinus applies the notion of "true lie" to a completely different context, that of the definition of matter; however, the reference to Plato's *Republic* is not misplaced. What Plotinus wants to convey by resorting to this Platonic expression is, first, that there is no truth whatsoever in matter, as matter is not an appearance that conceals a hidden truth. Moreover, as we learn from I.8.4, by adhering too deeply to matter, the soul fills itself with falsity and obscurity: matter is, therefore, a "true lie," also in the sense that it is the source and occasion for the deception, ignorance, and vice of the soul. Matter, indeed, is both the cause of the descent of the individual souls into bodies, which Plotinus depicts at the same time as a duty and as a sin of the soul (IV.8.4–5), and the occasion and source of the soul's evil acts, once the soul is embodied. Although matter as such does not do anything, as it is incapable of acting, its very existence has some crucial and negative effects on the soul. It compels the soul to descend, in order to take care of it, to give life and form to what is lifeless and formless, and in this way it provides the soul with the occasion for developing a desire to belong to itself and to separate itself from the whole intelligible reality in which the soul is free and happy: IV.8.4, 10–12. Finally, once the soul is embodied, matter is the source of its troubles: "If then the body is the cause of evils, matter would be in this way too the cause of evils. But, someone else might say, we have to get the better of it. But that which could get the better of it is not in a pure state unless it escapes. And the passions are stronger because of a corresponding mixture of bodies, and some people's passions are stronger than others', so that the individual's power cannot get the better of them, and some people have their powers of judgment dulled because bodily badness has chilled and restricted them; the opposite vices of bodily constitution make them unstable" (I.8.8, 27–34, translation: Armstrong).

5, 24 *This is the . . . "real non-being"*: *Ontōs mē on*, see Plato, *Sophist* 254d1. For the distinction between the different kinds of non-being in Plato's *Sophist* and in the *Enneads*, see above (*Commentary* 5.9–10).

5, 28–29 *so that, having . . . being in non-being*: The being of matter consists, as we have already seen, in its being a negation, namely the negation of being. This is the only kind of existence that belongs to it. It is true that in other treatises Plotinus seems to attribute some form of agency to matter, for example in III.6.14, 5–15, where Plotinus speaks of the frustrated attempts of matter-Penia to grab by an act of force the images coming from above, and of its restlessness; or in I.8.14, 35–36, where matter-evil is described as a kind of stalker of the soul: "and matter is there, and begs it and, we may say, bothers it and wants to come right inside" (translation: Armstrong). These expressions, however, should be taken only metaphorically: they indicate the role played by matter, viewed from the vantage point of the effects of its passive existence both on the constitution of sensible bodies and on the soul. From the viewpoint of the weakening of the *logoi* that become tridimensional by being projected upon matter and from the viewpoint of the soul which is filled with ignorance and obscurity due to its embodiment, matter does seem to be an agent. This, however, is only an appearance, as matter has not only no active power, but as Plotinus clarifies in VI.7.28, 8–9, it has neither desires nor sense-perception.

5, 32 *existence*: The word for existence is *hupostasis*. As noted by Narbonne (1998, 61), *hupostasis* does not have in Plotinus the technical meaning it will acquire with Porphyry, who will use *hupostasis* to refer to the three intelligible realities hierarchically organized within Plotinus' metaphysical system. In the *Enneads*, *hupostasis* usually indicates existence or the fact of being something real, namely a reality distinguished from its source.

5, 33–34 *If then it . . . matter as indestructible*: The impossibility of the corruption of matter is restated also in III.6.8, 11–12, where Plotinus consistently denies that matter has affections: having affections, indeed, would entail being subject to corruption. While bodies do have affections and, therefore, can undergo change and be destroyed, this is not the case for their underlying matter. By asserting the indestructibility of matter, Plotinus follows Plato, *Timaeus*

52a8–b1, where Timaeus explains that there is a third kind after intelligible reality and sensible reality, namely space (*chōra*), which is eternal and is not subject to destruction. The indestructibility of matter is maintained by Aristotle as well, in *Physics* 192a. In this passage Aristotle criticizes the Platonic identification between matter and privation and explains that in one sense matter is subject to corruption, while in another sense it is not. Indeed, if matter is the substrate and privation is its accident, in a process of change what is corrupted is the accidental privation that pertains to matter. If something ugly is changed into something beautiful, it is true that there is a corruption taking place within matter, but this corruption affects only the ugliness, that is, the privation of beauty, which was accidentally in the substrate and which disappears as an outcome of the process of change. But matter itself is not corrupted: it is not generated and is not destroyed. As noted by Kalligas (2014, *ad loc.*), the indestructibility of matter was firmly established as a sort of dogma as early as in the period of Middle Platonism.

In the conclusive lines of II.5, Plotinus addresses a direct challenge to the Aristotelians: "So, as it seems, it is necessary to say that it is only in potentiality, so that it may be what it is, unless one can refute these arguments." Aristotle was concerned with distinguishing between matter and privation so as to grant incorruptibility to matter. In Plotinus' view, this is a false reasoning and the consequence of Aristotle's own inconsistency concerning the *dunamis* of matter. Indeed, if we accept that matter can be affected, then we must also accept—on Aristotelian grounds—that matter can be corrupted and destroyed. Aristotle himself clarifies that we must call impassible that reality that does not have the principle of its own destruction either in something else or in itself as something else (*Metaphysics* 1019b11; see also Narbonne 1998, 61). The Aristotelians want both to assert that matter can be affected, since they maintain that matter changes from potentiality to actuality, and that matter cannot be destroyed. The two claims, however, are incompatible. This is why it is much more coherent to maintain that matter is privation and mere potential being, that it has its being in this real non-being, and that for this reason matter is also impassible: it cannot receive affections, it cannot be actualized, and it cannot undergo any change. Therefore, it is indestructible. In this way Plotinus breaks the Aristotelian correspondence between potentiality and actuality. Matter is a merely potential being that does not correspond to any actuality.

Select Bibliography

I. Ancient Authors

ALEXANDER OF APHRODISIAS: Hayduck, Michael, ed. 1891. *Alexandri Aphrodisiensis. In Aristotelis Metaphysica Commentaria*. Berlin: Reimer.

ALEXANDER OF APHRODISIAS: Sharples, Robert W., ed. 1992. *Alexander of Aphrodisias. Quaestiones 1.1–2.15*. Ithaca: Cornell University Press.

ALEXANDER OF APHRODISIAS: Sharples, Robert W., ed. 1992. *Alexander of Aphrodisias. Quaestiones 2.16–3.15*. Ithaca: Cornell University Press.

ARISTOTLE: Ross, William David, ed. 1925. *Aristotle's Metaphysics*. 2 vols. Oxford: Clarendon Press.

ARISTOTLE: Joachim, Harold H., ed. 1926. *Aristotle, On Coming-To-Be and Passing-Away* (*De Generatione and Corruptione*). Oxford: Clarendon Press.

ARISTOTLE: Ross, William David, ed. 1936. *Aristotle's Physics*. Oxford: Clarendon Press.

ARISTOTLE: Minio-Paluello, Lorenzo. 1949. *Aristotelis Categoriae et Liber de Interpretatione*. Oxford: Clarendon Press.

ARISTOTLE: Ross, William David, ed. 1955. *Aristotle: Parva Naturalia*. Oxford: Clarendon Press.

ARISTOTLE: Hett, Walter Stanley, ed. 1957. *Aristotle. On the Soul, Parva Naturalia, On Breath*. Cambridge, MA and London: Harvard University Press (Loeb).

ARISTOTLE: Ross, William David, ed. 1961. *Aristotle. De Anima*. Oxford: Clarendon Press.

ARISTOTLE: Moraux, Paul. 1965. *Aristote, Du ciel* (*De Caelo = On the Heavens*). Paris: Les Belles Lettres (Collection Budé).

ARISTOTLE: Ross, William David, trans. 1995. *Metaphysics*. In *The Complete Works of Aristotle. The Revised Oxford Translation*. Edited by Jonathan Barnes. Vol. 2, 1552–1728. Princeton: Princeton University Press.

ARISTOTLE: Hardie, Robert Purves and Russell Kerr Gaye. 1995. *Physics*. In *The Complete Works of Aristotle, The Revised Oxford Translation*. Vol. 1. Edited by Jonathan Barnes. Princeton: Princeton University Press.

NUMENIUS: des Places, Édouard, ed. 1973. *Numénius. Fragments*. Paris: Les Belles Lettres.

PLATO: Burnet, John, ed. 1900–1907. *Platonis Opera*. Oxford: Oxford University Press.

PLATO: Bloom, Allan, trans. 1991. *The Republic of Plato*. New York: Basic Books.

PLATO: Duke, E. A., W. F. Hicken, W. S. M. Nicoll, D. B. Robinson, and J. C. G. Strachan, eds. 1995. *Sophista*. In *Platonis Opera*. Vol. 1. Oxford: Oxford University Press.

PLATO: White, Nicholas P., trans. 1997. *Sophist*. In *Plato. Complete Works*. Edited by John M. Cooper, 235–293. Indianapolis/Cambridge: Hackett Publishing Company.

SIMPLICIUS: Diels, Hermann, ed. 1882. *Simplicii in Aristotelis Physicorum. Libros Quattuor Priores Commentaria*. Vol. IX. Berlin: Reimer.

II. Editions and Translations of the *Enneads*

Armstrong, Arthur Hilary. 1966–1982. *Plotinus, Enneads*. Greek Text with English Translation and Introductions. Cambridge, MA: Loeb.

Bréhier, Émile. 1924–1938. *Plotin, Ennéades*. Greek Text and French Translation with Introductions and Notes. Paris: Les Belles Lettres.

Casaglia, Mario, Chiara Guidelli, Alessandro Linguiti, and Fausto Moriani. 1997. *Enneadi di Plotino*. Italian Translation. Turin: Utet.

Cilento, Vincenzo. *Plotino, Enneadi*. Italian Translation and Commentary. Bari: Laterza.

Creuzer, Georg Friedrich. 1835. *Plotini Enneades*. Greek Text, with Marsilio Ficino's Latin Translation and Commentary. Oxford: E Typographeo Academico.

Dufour, Richard, Jérôme Laurent, and Laurent Lavaud. 2004. *Traités 22–26*. In *Plotin, Ennéades*. Directed by Luc Brisson and Jean François Pradeau. French Translation and Introduction. Paris: Flammarion.

Fleet, Barrie. 2012. *Plotinus. Ennead IV.8. On the Descent of the Soul into Bodies*. Translation, Introduction, Commentary. Las Vegas, Zurich, Athens: Parmenides Publishing.

Harder, Richard, Robert Beutler, and Willy Theiler. 1956–1971. Greek Text with German Translation and Commentary. *Plotins Schriften*. Hamburg: Meiner.

Henry, Paul and Hans-Rudolph Schwyzer. 1951–1973. *Plotini Opera* I–III (editio maior). Paris: Desclée de Brouwer et Cie (HS_1).

———. 1964–1982. *Plotini Opera* I–III (editio minor, with revised text). Oxford: Clarendon Press (HS_2).

Igal, Jesus. 1982–1988. *Porfirio, Vida de Plotino. Plotino, Enéadas I–II.* Introduction, Translations and Notes. Madrid: Gredos.

Kalligas, Paul. 2014. *The* Enneads *of Plotinus. A Commentary, Volume I.* Translated by E. K. Fowden and N. Pilavachi. Princeton and Oxford: Princeton University Press.

Kirchhoff, Adolph. 1856. *Plotini Opera.* Leipzig: Teubner.

MacKenna, Stephen. 1962[3]. *Plotinus: The Enneads.* English Translation Revised by B. S. Page. London: Faber & Faber.

———. 1991. *Plotinus. The Enneads.* Selected Treatises Revised with Notes by John Dillon. London: Penguin.

Narbonne, Jean-Marc. 1993. *Plotin. Les deux matières [Ennéades II, 4 (12)]. Introduction, Greek Text, French Translation, and Commentary.* Paris: Vrin.

———. 1998. *Plotin. Traité 25. Introduction, French Translation, Commentary, and Notes.* Paris: Les éditions du Cerf.

Perdikouri, Eleni. 2014. *Plotin. Traité 12. Introduction, French Translation, Commentary, and Notes.* Paris: Les éditions du Cerf.

III. Studies on *Ennead* II.5 and Related Works

Arruzza, Cinzia. 2011. "Passive Potentiality in the Physical Realm: Plotinus' Critique of Aristotle in *Enneads* II 5 [25]." *Archiv für Geschichte der Philosophie* 1, 24–57.

Aubry, Gwenäelle. 2000. "Puissance et principe: la *dunamis pantōn* ou puissance de tout." *Kairos* 15, 9–32.

———. 2006. *Dieu sans la puissance. Dunamis et Energeia chex Aristote et chez Plotin.* Paris: Vrin.

Blumenthal, Henry. 1971. "Soul, World Soul, and Individual Soul in Plotinus." In *Le Néoplatonisme.* Edited by Pierre Maxime, M. Schuhl, and Pierre Hadot, 55–66. Paris: CNRS.

Brisson, Luc. 2008. "La définition de l'être par la puissance. Un commentaire de *Sophiste* 247B-249D." In Dunamis. *Autour de la puissance chez Aristote.* Edited by Michel Crubellier, Annick Jaulin, David Lefebvre, and Pierre-Marie Morel, 173–186. Louvain-La-Neuve: Éditions Peeters.

Buchner, Hans. 1970. *Plotins Möglichkeitslehre.* München: Verlag Anton Pustet.

Brunschwig, Jacques. 2003. "Stoic Metaphysics." In *The Cambridge Companion to the Stoics.* Edited by Brad Inwood, 206–232. Cambridge: Cambridge University Press.

Chiaradonna, Riccardo. 2002. *Sostanza, movimento, analogia. Plotino critico di Aristotele*. Naples: Bibliopolis.

———. 2008. "*Energeia* et *kinēsis* chez Plotin et Aristote (*Enn*. VI 1, [42], 16, 4–19)." In Dunamis. *Autour de la puissance chez Aristote*, edited by Michel Crubellier, Annick Jaulin, David Lefebvre, and Pierre-Marie Morel, 471–491. Louvain-La-Neuve: Éditions Peeters.

Cleary John, J. 2013. "The Concept of Potency in Plato and Aristotle." In *Studies on Plato, Aristotle, and Proclus. The Collected Essays on Ancient Philosophy of John Cleary*. Edited by John Dillon, Brendan O'Byrne, and Fran O'Rourke, 251–297. Leiden: Brill.

Corrigan, Kevin. 1986. "Is There More than One Generation of Matter in the *Enneads*?" *Phronesis* 30, 167–181.

———. 1996. *Plotinus' Theory of Matter-Evil and the Question of Substance in Plato, Aristotle, and Alexander of Aphrodisias*. Leuven: Peeters.

Dixsaut, Monique. 1991. "La négation, le non-être et l'autre dans le *Sophiste*." In *Études sur le Sophiste de Platon*. Edited by Michel Narcy, 167–213. Naples: Bibliopolis.

Dufour, Richard. 2004. "Actuality and Potentiality in Plotinus' View of the Intelligible Universe." *Journal of Neoplatonic Studies* 9/2, 193–218.

Emilsson, Eyjólfur K. 1988. *Plotinus on Sense-Perception. A Philosophical Study*. Cambridge, New York, Melbourne, Sidney: Cambridge University Press.

———. 2007. *Plotinus on Intellect*. Oxford: Clarendon Press.

Fronterotta, Francesco. 2001. *Methexis. La teoria platonica delle idee e la partecipazione delle cose empiriche: dai dialoghi giovanili al* Parmenide. Pisa: Scuola Normale Superiore.

———. 2008. "La notion de *dunamis* dans le *Sophiste* de Platon: *koinōnia* entre les formes et methexis du sensible à l'intelligible." In Dunamis. *Autour de la puissance chez Aristote*. Edited by Michel Crubellier, Annick Jaulin, David Lefebvre, and Pierre-Marie Morel, 187–224. Louvain-La-Neuve: Éditions Peeters.

Gerson, Lloyd. 1994. *Plotinus*. London: Routledge.

Gill, Mary Louise. 2008. "Form-Matter predication in *Metaphysics* Θ 7." In Dunamis. *Autour de la puissance chez Aristote*. Edited by Michel Crubellier, Annick Jaulin, David Lefebvre, and Pierre-Marie Morel, 391–427. Louvain-La-Neuve: Éditions Peeters.

Happ, Heinz. 1971. *Hyle. Studien zum aristotelischen Materie-Begriff*. Berlin, New York: de Gruyter.

Horn Christoph. 2003. "L'auto-déclaration de l'Un dans l'*Ennéade* V, 3 [49] et son arrière-plan dans la théorie plotinienne de la predication." In *La connaissance de soi. Études sur le traité 49 de Plotin*, edited by Monique Dixsaut, 41–71. Paris: Vrin.

Kalligas, Pavlos. 1997. "Logos and the Sensible Object in Plotinus." *Ancient Philosophy* 17, 397–410.

———. 2011. "The Structure of Appearances: Plotinus on the Constitution of Sensible Objects." *The Philosophical Quarterly* 61/245, 762–782.

Lee, Edward N. 1972. "Plato on Negation and Not-Being in the *Sophist*." *The Philosophical Review* 71, 267–304.

Linguiti, Alessandro. 2007. "La materia dei corpi: sullo pseudoilemorfismo plotiniano." *Quaestio* 7, 105–122.

Menn, Stephen. 1994. "The Origins of Aristotle's Concept of *Energeia*: *Energeia* and *Dynamis*." *Ancient Philosophy* 14, 73–114.

Narbonne, Jean-Marc. 1992. "Le non-être chez Plotin et dans la tradition grecque." *Revue de philosophie ancienne* 10, 115–33.

———. 2006. "Plotinus and the Gnostic on the Generation of Matter (33 [II 9], 12 and 51 [I 8], 14)." *Dionysius* 24, 45–64.

———. 2007. "La controverse à propos de la génération de la matière chez Plotin: l'énigme résolue?" *Quaestio* 7, 123–263.

Natali, Carlo. 2008. "*Dynamis* e *techne* nel pensiero di Aristotele." In Dunamis. *Autour de la puissance chez*

Aristote. Edited by Michel Crubellier, Annick Jaulin, David Lefebvre, and Pierre-Marie Morel, 271–290. Louvain-La-Neuve: Éditions Peeters.

Noble, Christopher. 2013. “Plotinus’ Unaffectable Matter.” *Oxford Studies in Ancient Philosophy* 44, 233–277.

O’Brien, Denis. 1991. *Plotinus on the Origin of Matter. An Exercise in the Interpretation of the Enneads*. Naples: Bibliopolis.

Pigler A. 2008. “L’ Aristote de Plotin. Sur le problème de la puissance et de l’acte dans le traité 25 (II, 5).” In *Mélanges de philosophie et de philologie offerts à Lambros Couloubaritsis*. Edited by M. Broze, B. Decharneux and S. Delcomminette, 503–516. Paris: Vrin.

Smith, Andrew. 1981. “Potentiality and the Problem of Plurality in the Intelligible World.” In *Neoplatonism and Early Christian Thought*. Edited by Henry J. Blumenthal and Robert A. Markus, 99–107. London: Variorum Publications.

Taormina, Daniela Patrizia. 1999. *Jamblique, critique de Plotin et de Porphyre*. Paris: Vrin.

Tornau, Christian. 1998. “Wissenschaft, Seele, Geist. Zur Bedeutung einer Analogie bei Plotin (*Ennead* IV 9, 5 und VI 2, 20).” *Göttinger Forum für Altertumswissenschaft* 1, 87–111.

Wildberg, Christian. 2009. "A World of Thoughts: Plotinus on Nature and Contemplation. *Enn.* III 8 [30] 1–6." In *Physics and Philosophy of Nature in Greek Neoplatonism. Proceedings of the European Science Foundation Exploratory Workshop.* Edited by Riccardo Chiaradonna and Franco Trabattoni, 121–144. Leiden: Brill.

IV. General Publications

Alt, K. 1993. *Weltflucht und Weltbejahung. Zur Frage des Leib-Seele Dualismus bei Plutarch, Numenius, Plotin.* Stuttgart: Franz Steiner Verlag.

Armstrong, A. H. 1940. *The Architecture of the Intelligible Universe in the Philosophy of Plotinus.* Cambridge: Cambridge University Press.

———, ed. 1967. *The Cambridge History of Later Greek and Early Medieval Philosophy.* Cambridge: Cambridge University Press.

Arnou, R. 1968. *Le Désir de Dieu dans la philosophie de Plotin.* 2nd ed. Rome: Presses de l'Université Grégorienne.

Dillon, J. 1977/1996. *The Middle Platonists: A Study of Platonism, 80 B.C.–A.D. 220,* London: Duckworth.

Dodds, Eric R. 1965. *Pagan and Christian in an Age of Anxiety: Some Aspects of Religious Experience from Marcus Aurelius to Constantine*. Cambridge: Cambridge University Press.

Emilsson, Eyjólfur K. 1988. *Plotinus on Sense-Perception. A Philosophical Study*. Cambridge, New York, Melbourne, Sidney: Cambridge University Press.

———. 2007. *Plotinus on Intellect*. Oxford: The Clarendon Press.

Gatti, M. L. 1996. *Plotino e la metafisica della contemplazione*, Milan: Vita e Pensiero.

Gerson, L. P. 1994. *Plotinus*, London/New York: Routledge.

———, ed. 1996. *The Cambridge Companion to Plotinus*, Cambridge: Cambridge University Press.

———, ed. 2010. *The Cambridge History of Philosophy in Late Antiquity*. 2 vols. Cambridge: Cambridge University Press.

Gottschalk, H. B. 1980. *Heraclides of Pontus*. Oxford: Oxford University Press.

Guthrie, W. K. C. 1967–1978. *A History of Greek Philosophy*, 5 vols. Cambridge: Cambridge University Press.

Hadot, Pierre. 1993. *Plotinus on the Simplicity of Vision*. Translated by M. Chase. Chicago: Chicago University Press.

Inge, W. R. 1948. *The Philosophy of Plotinus*. 3rd ed. London: Longmans, Green.

Les Sources de Plotin, 1960. Entretiens Fondation Hardt V. Vandoeuvres-Genève.

Lloyd, Anthony C. 1990. *The Anatomy of Neoplatonism.* Oxford: Clarendon Press.

Meijer, P. A. 1992. *Plotinus on the Good or the One (Enneads VI, 9): An Analytical Commentary*, Amsterdam: J. C. Gieben.

O'Daly, G. 1973. *Plotinus' Philosophy of the Self*, Irish University Press: Shannon.

O'Meara, Dominic J., 1993. *Plotinus: an Introduction to the Enneads.* Oxford: Oxford University Press.

Pépin, J. 1958. *Mythe et allégorie: les origins grecques et les contestations judéo-chrétiennes.* Paris: Aubier.

Remes, Pauliina. 2007. *Plotinus on Self: The Philosophy of the 'We.'* Cambridge: Cambridge University Press.

———. 2008. *Neoplatonism.* Berkeley: University of California Press.

Rist, John M., 1967. *Plotinus: The Road to Reality.* Cambridge: Cambridge University Press.

Schniewind, Alexandrine. 2003. *L'Éthique du Sage chez Plotin.* Paris: J. Vrin.

Smith, A. 1974. *Porphyry's Place in the Neoplatonic Tradition: A Study in Post-Plotinian Neoplatonism*, The Hague: Nijhoff.

———. 1981. "Potentiality and the Problem of Plurality in the Intelligible," in *Neoplatonism and Early Christian Thought*, eds. H. J. Blumenthal and R. A. Markus. London: Variorum, 99–107.

———. 2004. *Philosophy in Late Antiquity.* London: Routledge.

Theiler, W. 1960. "Plotin zwischen Platon und Stoa." In *Les Sources de Plotin*. Entretiens Fondation Hardt V. Vandoeuvres-Genève: Fondation Hardt, 63–103.

Wallis, R. T. 1995. *Neoplatonism.* 2nd ed. London: Duckworth.

West, M. L. 1966. *Hesiod* Theogony, *Edited with Prolegomena and Commentary.* Oxford: Clarendon Press.

Index of Ancient Authors

Index of Names and Subjects

PRE-SOCRATICS

By Being, It Is: *The Thesis of Parmenides* by Néstor-Luis Cordero

The Fragments of *Parmenides*: *A Critical Text with Introduction and Translation, the Ancient Testimonia and a Commentary by A. H. Coxon. Revised and Expanded Edition edited with new Translations by Richard McKirahan and a new Preface* by Malcolm Schofield

The Legacy of Parmenides: *Eleatic Monism and Later Presocratic Thought* by Patricia Curd

Parmenides and the History of Dialectic: *Three Essays* by Scott Austin

Parmenides, Venerable and Awesome: *Proceedings of the International Symposium* edited by Néstor-Luis Cordero

Presocratics and Plato: *A Festschrift in Honor of Charles Kahn* edited by Richard Patterson, Vassilis Karasmanis, and Arnold Hermann

The Route of Parmenides: *Revised and Expanded Edition, With a New Introduction, Three Supplemental Essays, and an Essay* by Gregory Vlastos by Alexander P. D. Mourelatos

To Think Like God: *Pythagoras and Parmenides. The Origins of Philosophy. Scholarly and fully annotated edition* by Arnold Hermann

The Illustrated To Think Like God: *Pythagoras and Parmenides. The Origins of Philosophy* by Arnold Hermann (with over 200 full color illustrations)

PLATO

The Second Alcibiades: *A Platonist Dialogue on Prayer and on Ignorance* by Harold Tarrant

A Stranger's Knowledge: *Statesmanship, Philosophy, and Law in Plato's Statesman* by Xavier Márquez

God and Forms in Plato by Richard D. Mohr

Image and Paradigm in Plato's Sophist by David Ambuel

Imperial Plato: Albinus, Maximus, Apuleius by Ryan Fowler

Interpreting Plato's Dialogues by J. Angelo Corlett

One Book, the Whole Universe: *Plato's Timaeus Today* edited by Richard D. Mohr and Barbara M. Sattler

Platonic Patterns: *A Collection of Studies* by Holger Thesleff

Plato's Late Ontology: *A Riddle Resolved* by Kenneth M. Sayre

Plato's Parmenides: *Text, Translation & Introductory Essay* by Arnold Hermann. Translation in collaboration with Sylvana Chrysakopoulou with a Foreword by Douglas Hedley

Plato's Universe by Gregory Vlastos

The Philosopher in Plato's Statesman by Mitchell Miller

ARISTOTLE

Aristotle's Empiricism: Experience and Mechanics in the Fourth Century B.C. by Jean De Groot

One and Many in Aristotle's Metaphysics—*Volume I: Books Alpha-Delta* by Edward C. Halper

One and Many in Aristotle's Metaphysics—*Volume 2: The Central Books* by Edward C. Halper

Reading Aristotle: Physics VII.3 "What is Alteration?" *Proceedings of the International ESAP-HYELE Conference* edited by Stefano Maso, Carlo Natali, and Gerhard Seel

HELLENISTIC PHILOSOPHY

A Life Worthy of the Gods: *The Materialist Psychology of Epicurus* by David Konstan

THE *ENNEADS* OF PLOTINUS

Translations with Introductions & Philosophical Commentaries
Series edited by John M. Dillon and Andrew Smith

Ennead* I.1: *What Is the Living Thing? What Is Man? by Gerard O'Daly

Ennead* I.6: *On Beauty by Andrew Smith

Ennead* II.9: *Against the Gnostics by Sebastian Ramon Philipp Gertz

Ennead* II.4: *On Matter by Anthony A. Long

Ennead* III.4: *On Our Allotted Guardian Spirit by Wiebke-Marie Stock

Ennead* IV.3–IV.4.29: *Problems concerning the Soul by John M. Dillon and H. J. Blumenthal

Ennead* IV.4.30–45 & IV.5: *Problems concerning the Soul by Gary M. Gurtler

Ennead* IV.7: *On the Immortality of the Soul by Barrie Fleet

Ennead* IV.8: *On the Descent of the Soul into Bodies by Barrie Fleet

Ennead* V.1: *On the Three Primary Levels of Reality by Eric D. Perl

Ennead* V.5: *That the Intelligibles are not External to the Intellect, and on the Good by Lloyd P. Gerson

Ennead* VI.4 & VI.5: *On the Presence of Being, One and the Same, Everywhere as a Whole by Eyjólfur Emilsson and Steven Strange

Ennead* VI.8: *On the Voluntary and on the Free Will of the One by Kevin Corrigan and John D. Turner

Ennead* VI.9: *On the Good or the One by Stephen R. L. Clark

ETHICS

Sentience and Sensibility: *A Conversation about Moral Philosophy* by Matthew R. Silliman

PHILOSOPHICAL FICTION

Pythagorean Crimes by Tefcros Michaelides

The Aristotle Quest: A Dana McCarter Trilogy. Book 1: Black Market Truth by Sharon M. Kaye

AUDIOBOOKS

The Iliad (unabridged) by Stanley Lombardo

The Odyssey (unabridged) by Stanley Lombardo

The Essential Homer by Stanley Lombardo

The Essential Iliad by Stanley Lombardo

FORTHCOMING

Ennead I.2: ***On Virtues*** by Suzanne Stern-Gillet

Ennead I.3: ***On Dialectic*** by Pauliina Remes

Ennead I.4: ***On Well-Being*** by Kieran McGroarty

Ennead I.5: ***On Whether Well-Being Increases with Time*** by Danielle A. Laney

Ennead I.8: ***On the Nature and Source of Evil*** by Anne Sheppard

Ennead I.9: ***On Going Out of the Body*** by Suzanne Stern-Gilet

Ennead II.1: ***On the Heavens by*** Andrew Smith

Ennead II.6: ***On Substance, or On Quality*** by Damien Caluori

Ennead II.7: ***On Complete Blending*** by Robert Goulding

Ennead II.8: ***On Sight*** by Robert Goulding

Ennead III.5: ***On Love*** by Sara Magrin

Ennead III.6: ***On Impassibility*** by Eleni Perdikouri

Ennead III.7: ***On Eternity and Time*** by László Bene

Ennead III.8: ***On Nature and Contemplation*** by George Karamanolis

Ennead IV.6: ***On Sense-Perception and Memory*** by Peter Lautner

Ennead IV.9: ***If All Souls are One*** by Eyjólfur Emilsson

Ennead V.2, V.4, and V.6: ***On the One and Intellect*** by Eleni Perdikouri

Ennead V.3: ***On the Knowing Hypostases*** by Marie-Élise Zovko

Ennead V.9: ***On Intellect, Ideas, and Being*** by Matthias Vorwerk

Ennead VI.1-2: ***On the Genera of Being (I+II)*** by Damien Caluori and Regina Füchslin

Ennead VI.3: ***On the Genera of Being (III)*** by Riccardo Chiaradonna

Ennead VI.7: ***The Forms and the Good*** by Nicholas Banner